Credit Basics Training

Eye-Opening Revelations to Change your Life for the Better

Christine Foster

authorHOUSE®

AuthorHouse™
1663 Liberty Drive, Suite 200
Bloomington, IN 47403
www.authorhouse.com
Phone: 1-800-839-8640

First published by AuthorHouse 6/2/2008

Printed in the United States of America
Bloomington, Indiana
This book is printed on acid-free paper.
ISBN: 978-1-4343-7558-2 (sc)

Library of Congress Control Number: 2008903283

Syllabus

In this book we describe some of the different types of loans available in the marketplace. An overview of information about financial services is provided so that you can select a program you feel best services your financial situation. Many of the rules and regulations that the financial institutions must abide by are defined. There is a section that discusses some of the pitfalls to avoid when entering into a financial transaction and one on how to maintain your debt. There is also a section that will give you some information about credit bureau reports and the credit bureau agencies. One that explains what happens to your credit when your debt is out of control or you have a financially difficult time. There is also an overview of what the financial institution can and cannot do.

What Is Credit All About?

There are times in everyone's life when they would like to purchase something but they do not have the cash to purchase it. In such cases there is an alternative: You can enter into a financial credit transaction. There are many types of loans and many ways for financial institutions to make money on your transaction. There is of course an acceptable level of cost associated with any financial transaction. The key is to understand loans and some of the terminology so that you can make an educated decision. A simple credit transaction involves borrowing an amount of money in order to purchase something or spend money on something that you normally could not afford to purchase without the loan. This loan is typically set up on a repayment term or monthly payment. There is usually a length of time determined that the debt will be outstanding, which is the term of the loan, for example 2, 3, 5, 10, 15,20, 30 years. There are many other features that we will also discuss, such as types of interest, adjustable or fixed, that will enhance your financial knowledge.

What Happens When I Can't Pay?

There are situations for many of us when our lives are out of our control. Many times people enter into a financial transaction and are fully prepared to repay the debt as agreed. Then later they become unemployed or have a medical or a family situation that does not enable them to repay their debt as agreed. Later in this book we provide information that you need to know in order for you to be prepared for those situations.

How Do I Maintain My Debt?

Within this book there is information for you to use to be able to plan a budget and better understand your credit.

What Regulations and Rules Apply to Credit?

There are many regulations that financial institutions must follow in order to protect themselves and the consumer. We provide definitions and explanations of when those rules apply and Information on whom to speak with if you feel that you have been taken advantage of or if you think there has been wrong doing within the financial market. We also provide you with resource information so that you can do further research.

Table of Contents

Section 1 Credit Options
Chapter 1:

Types of Loans

As always make sure you know what you are signing and what the documents tell you. We dedicate a chapter to all types of documents and fees later in the book. We also discuss the different types of loans and how they are closed .

Mortgage Loans

You may obtain a loan that is secured with a lien, also known as giving security interest on a property you currently own, or obtain a loan for a property you intend to purchase. When you purchase a home with the funds from the lender, it is considered a purchase money loan or residential loan. You may decide to combine the balance you already owe on your home with additional funds for home improvement, debt consolidation, student education, and various other expenses. If you decide to combine your current need with the balance you already owe, then you would be refinancing your home. There are things you might want to accomplish, you might decide that you simply want to refinance your home to improve your interest rate, terms, or loan to value considerations. Loan to value is the amount you owe as it relates to the value of your home or the ratio of amount owed versus home value. If you only refinance to alter your terms and there is no additional funds added to the loan then this type of loan is usually considered a streamline refinance because your mortgage company normally would not charge you all the usual fees. Since you are just refinancing to improve your interest rate, typically no appraisal is required, or maybe simply a title work charge. In either case you would be obtaining a first mortgage lien against your home. You may also decide that you do not want to touch your first mortgage balance and the terms you currently have on your home, but instead you would like to take out a second mortgage for the funds you currently need. This choice may be made based on the fact that you have paid an enormous amount on your principal and it doesn't make sense at that point to refinance the entire balance. We discuss this further later in the book so that you can understand the reasoning. This second mortgage option is usually considered a home equity loan, meaning that there is a first lien outstanding on your home and the new lender will be placed in second position behind your first mortgage. If something were to happen, the second mortgage is second in line to collect. There are also third liens, but this type of lending is rare and typically expensive for the home owner. You can also purchase a second home, which you could consider for a vacation home or investment rental property. Now let's say you have found your dream home, but you haven't sold your current home yet. You could use your current "owned" property in order to purchase the other property you intend to move into by acquiring a bridge loan. A bridge loan is typically only available for someone who has been living in their home for enough time to build up equity in the home. When you own your home and have been paying if off for some time, you begin to build what is called equity in the home. Additionally, in most communities the value of homes increases. This is called appreciation.

How is equity acquired? Say, for example, that you have owned your home for 10 years, purchased it for $100,000, put down $10,000, and have paid $10,000 towards the principal balance on your home loan, plus now your home is worth $150,000. So you took out an original $90,000 home loan minus the $10,000 you have paid into principal. Now you owe $80,000 and your home is worth $150,000 ($150,000 − $80,000 = $70,000), so you have $70,000 in equity. Now you would like to upgrade to a larger and more expensive home. You need that equity in order to meet the down payment requirements, but you have not sold your home yet, or the sale is pending. You can take out a bridge loan for a portion of that equity; you shouldn't mortgage 100 percent of the value in your home, as you may not sell the home for the exact amount it is worth. Make sure to consider closing costs and commission fees associated with the closing. A bridge loan could be for that portion you intend to use as a down payment on your new home. The terms of this loan should be reviewed carefully, as the intention should be temporary use of these funds until you are able to sell your other home. Do not take out this type of loan if you are not certain your home will sell within a reasonable amount of time. There are several ways lenders structure these loans— with deferral payments or interest-only payments—or they set up the plan for only six months at a time. Once that time is up they may allow you to redo the loan or extend the repayment period on the contract. We will talk about these items later. But this type of lending is risky and especially risky for the consumer. You are taking on two house payments, so it is something to consider carefully.

What are the differences between lien positions for mortgages or mortgages on different types of property ownership? Well, all mortgages have a claim or lien to/on your home; however, the second mortgage company and the lender for the rental or vacation property do not have a first claim to the home you live in, so for business purposes they are riskier loans for the lender. In case of default or non-payment the second mortgage or subsequent liens must actually pay off any liens on the property before them in order to have a true claim to the property. Most second lien lenders simply elect to take the loss and allow the first to proceed with their foreclosure.

 From a lender's perspective you value the home you live in more than any other home you own, and of course your first priority would be your first mortgage on that home. The bridge loan is an even riskier loan than a first or second mortgage, as you could take the money you need to purchase the home you want and "walk away" from this type of loan, and not repay the debt. So if you do not pay on a first, second, or any other type of mortgage, the lender is left with recourse to foreclose on the home. But this is very expensive and time consuming, and since the lender is not in the business of selling homes, they would prefer to lend only to clients that are likely to repay their debts. We will discuss default and foreclosure later. Of course that would also create a bad credit situation, but in some cases this is an unavoidable occurrence once you have taken out the loan and you cannot sell your home or pay on the debt. Most mortgages potentially have a tax advantage, but seek advice from a tax professional to be sure.

A lien gives the holder (mortgage lender) the right to claim or reclaim the property for repayment of a debt. Many refer to a lien on a property as using the property for security. Basically, when you acquire a loan and use your property to secure the loan, the lender will place a lien on your property that you own or through the loan will own. This gives them the right to foreclose on this home for nonpayment, which we will discuss further in a later chapter of the book. For now you need to understand that when you take out a loan that places a lien on your home you need to be sure the transaction is the right one for you and that you have the ability to repay that debt. Planning is important, to repay this debt even if you come upon difficult times.

Typically, when you obtain a home purchase loan for the first time, it is likely that you will enlist the services that the realtor has at his/her disposal. The realtor can refer you to a bank he/she does business with regularly or a broker, who normally locates a lender to service your needs. Make sure you are represented well, either by your choice of an attorney or through your own research about the broker and or lender you intend to use. There are many types of loans that you can acquire, and once again later in the book we will outline those types for you. For now let's just discuss some of the terms that are available through the various types of lenders. Remember there is no true standard for lending throughout the United States or even abroad, and you have the right to review programs and shop around to the various lenders available to you.

For your first home purchase, in many cases you will not need to have a substantial down payment in order to obtain the home loan. There are programs available, for example, you pay zero down, paying only fees at closing; the key is to research the available programs and find the right one for you. Although there are no down payment programs, the fact that you were able to save enough for some down payment indicates you are more ready to become a homeowner. There are certain programs available to the first-time home owner. FHA (Federal Housing Administration) is a popular program that financial institutions use. This agency was created in 1934 by the National Housing Act and is now a part of the Department of Housing and Urban Development. The agency insures residential mortgages, for a certain amount, at prevailing rates. This program assists those who normally would not be able to obtain a conventional home loan and become home owners. There are many other types of assistance programs, but generally they are funded and monitored by Housing and Urban Development (HUD). Below is the web site so that you can research the types of programs they currently offer.

4

HUD web site:

http://www.hud.gov/offices/hsg/index.cfm

If you are not a first-time home buyer, in order to improve the terms for your loan, you may choose to use a conventional lender, with a down payment of at least 20 percent. When you only borrow 80 percent, it is typically considered a conventional loan and usually affords you a lower interest rate than if you were trying to finance 100 percent of the value of the home. Many lenders will not lend more than 80 percent, and the ones that do are usually consider sub-prime lenders or they have FHA insure the amount over 80 percent. The sub-prime lenders typically charge a surplus for that riskier loan, which also leads to one of the additional fees charged: Private Mortgage Insurance (PMI). PMI is insurance charged to the consumer for the mortgage company that covers any loan value over the 80 percent; see the fee section for a full definition. There are many other fees associated with mortgage loans: See the fee section for further information.

In summary, for mortgage loans, there are first liens, second liens, and so on. Subsections of those would be purchase money, refinances, streamlines, home equity, rental/vacation mortgage loans, and bridge loans. There are governmental assistance programs. There are prime and sub-prime lenders and brokers to consider. Now you have some basic knowledge about mortgage lending.

Prime vs. Sub-Prime

Mortgage Lending

What is New in Lending Today?

What is the difference between what you qualify for, would they consider it a sub-prime or a prime loan? Many institutions make loans of all different qualifications, while others specialize in lending just to the sub prime market, or just the prime market.

Prime

The type of lending for prime in many cases is much different than sub-prime . The loan to value—value of the home versus the lending amount—will be less since for prime lending they take less risk and offer lower interest rates. For example a customer that only needed to use 80 percent of their equity in their home would probably be considered prime based on collateral; however, the customer's credit history will also be a factor we will discuss later. If you elect to get a loan at say 90 percent of the value of your home, you will probably have to pay for Private Mortgage Insurance if you are getting a prime loan. PM insurance is a monthly fee, and in some cases it is tax deductible. PMI actually covers a portion of the lending balance in case of certain default reasons for the percentage of the loan the exceeds 80 percent. It works like most insurance policies except that it protects the lender and not the consumer. The main factors for qualifying for a prime loan are your credit score, credit history, assets, and loan to value of your home.

A prime customer might also qualify for government sponsored programs such as FHA or VA. (See links below.)

http://www.hud.gov/offices/hsg/sfh/insured.cfm

http://www.hud.gov/

These government-sponsored programs normally require certification to process; therefore they are normally only handled at banks under the prime division. These loans usually require more than an average loan for documentation; it takes longer to process these types of loans as well.

Typically a prime customer will have good to great credit and no mortgage late payments within the last 12 months. A prime customer normally has less debt versus their income. In other words they usually have more disposable income left over after they make their monthly payments. A prime customer might have more in liquid assets, such as cash, stocks, and bonds, that they could easily convert to cash. These factors all make this type of customer a lower risk for the lender, and therefore typically they will get a lower interest rate.

Sub-Prime

Sub-prime lending is a complicated business. This type of loan requires the lender to analyze the consumer to determine the probability of repayment. There are several factors that go into this, much like with prime lending. You would review each person's credit score and determine based on a comparison of the score and the type of loan that the consumer wants—loan to value and terms—if the lender is willing to take the risk. Ownership in the property is also a factor that must be considered. If the consumer just purchased the home, the lender must consider how much the borrower has to lose if, for example, they put money down on the property to purchase or pay for home improvements, etc. There are other types of properties as well, such as non-owner occupied, but since we are just dealing with the average consumer we won't get into that type of lending here. When we discuss risk it is because sub-prime lending is for the riskier loans versus prime loans. Most lenders have a matrix to follow and exception limits if the consumer does not fit into the box. Even prime lending has a matrix that determines if the consumer is not a prime customer and is in fact sub-prime. Compensating factors would need to be determined for exceptions to policy matrices, such as having additional assets, low loan to value, low debt to income ratio, high credit scores, a long-time job, and/or long time at the residence. Exception lending is very risky and may result in default, so it must be consider carefully. Let's remember that the lender will lose, but the consumer will also lose their home. Responsible lending is very important; in fact the government watches this activity carefully. After reviewing the matrix and the borrower's basics, the score, and the type of loan, then true underwriting must be done. One must look at the credit and determine if there is a certain time frame when an event occurred; they must also determine if the delinquency is sporadic or consist. As with anything, past performance can be an indicator of future results, but not in all cases. Sometimes consumers just had something happen that prevented them from making their monthly obligations versus not wanting to or not being organized enough to make them on time. Based on this analysis and the matrix, an underwriter will determine what the consumer qualifies for and possibly approve the loan for those terms.

For example, a loan application is submitted for 95 percent loan to value. The home is worth $100,000, and the consumer needs $95,000 in order to accomplish their needs. Let's say they currently owe $80,000 on the home and they have $10,000 in additional debt to pay off, which means they probably want $5,000 cash for other needs. The underwriter will review how they have made their mortgage payment—have they paid on time according to the credit bureau report. The underwriter will also review how long they have been in the home, how much they originally paid for the home, and whether the increase in value makes sense (sometimes the appraisal is complete and those questions can be answered at time of original underwriting). Let's assume that the underwriter believes in the value of the home, which is directly related to the risk factor since if the value is not there more is at risk. Let's also assume that the time in residence and at the job is within standards. Now that the value has been determined and we already know that the consumer wants 95 percent of the value, how much risk is there? Well, there is only $5,000 worth of value left on this home, and if the lender were to foreclose that isn't much to cover the costs of such an event. In this case the underwriter needs to be fairly certain this consumer will repay the debt or they are taking a lot of risk in approving this loan. If you take a different example such as a home worth $500,000 and lend 95 percent on that amount, which is $475,000, then you have $25,000 left over, a big dollar difference. Once the value has been determined, the underwriter will review the matrix to ensure the consumer qualifies for the 95 percent loan to value based on their credit score and terms of the loan (such as fixed-rate, 30-year term). Then the underwriter normally has to review the income documentation to ensure the proper figures are used to determine the debt load based on income versus debt. Let's say they get the $95,000 loan on a 30-year fixed interest rate at 8 percent; the payment would be around $697.00 without monthly real estate taxes and without monthly home owners' insurance. If their real estate taxes were $2,000 a year and their insurance coverage was $200 a year, then the monthly payment would be around $183. So in this case the total mortgage payments would be $880.00 a month, assuming that the lender didn't require PMI, which most sub-prime lenders do not. Let's say this borrower makes $5,000 a month in gross income and the only other payment after we pay off the $10,000 in debt described earlier is an auto payment of $500.00; then this customer would certainly be able to pay the $1,380.00 in monthly obligations left over after the loan is made. Therefore it is more likely that the loan will be approved.

You may have heard of the three C's of underwriting; Collateral—can the lender recover their money in case of default; Credit—what is the likelihood of repayment; and Capacity—is the consumer able to repay the debt. Each institution has its own version, but basically these are the main three.

To summarize, the lender must use a matrix that the business has used to determine the acceptable risk in evaluating each consumer. Both prime lending and sub-prime lending have their own parameters to follow in order to maintain quality and a certain level of acceptable risk and acceptable charges, but not excessive profit. If there is an exception to be made to policy, then there must be a reason, and fair lending as well as responsible lending should be considered.

Auto Loans

As with mortgages, auto loans are considered secured loans. But with this type of loan you are using your auto for security. You can have first and second liens for auto loans as well; it would be very rare to have a third lien. The same concept applies: The lender has the right to claim or reclaim the auto in case of nonpayment of the debt. Repossession is a much simpler process than foreclosure. The lender has certain paperwork to complete, but not typically a court case with a court order, and they could reclaim you car. As with mortgages you can use an auto loan to purchase a vehicle or you can refinance your current vehicle. The reasons for refinance might be to improve your terms, such as interest rate or lower monthly payments, or to get additional funds for a current need. There may be fees associated with this type of loan such as recording fees for the lender to record their lien on your auto title, or processing fees and recording stamps. Make sure you review your documents to ensure you are aware of which fees are being charged and for what. Auto dealerships have additional fees as well, and in many cases they are standard fees, but you should review for necessity. All fees should make sense. If, for example, there is a delivery charge for a vehicle that you picked out on the lot, you might want to ask why, since it wasn't delivered specifically for you, but rather delivered to them. That same charge may apply when you order a car with specifications that they don't have on the lot and of course may be acceptable on that basis. As with all loans watch the unneeded items, for example, if they offer you a warranty be sure the terms would be useful to you personally.

Personal Loans

For personal loans there is no pledge of substance for security. Instead a personal loan is secured with the consumer's signature or promise to repay. Because there is only the promise to repay instead of actual property, the funds the financial institution lends are not as safe, and therefore these loans are typically lent with higher interest rates and for a shorter amount of time. Personal loans are risky and would probably not be considered for someone who does not make their monthly payments, according to the credit bureau report. Many of these types of loans carry fees for processing the transaction, annual fees, and other fees. Some of these loans have additional agreements that go with them, such as a wage assignment. This document is usually not held to the highest standard, such as a court order for wages, but it can be executed against your payroll unless you protest in some legitimate way. Even though you have not pledged anything for security you should still be careful not to borrow unless you truly need to. If in fact you find yourself without the ability to pay even a personal loan, it can damage your credit extensively if not paid or not paid on time. A small loan can also "place" a lien on assets, even your home, through the court process.

Credit Cards

Credit cards are again secured with only the consumer's signature and promise to repay. In some cases, the creditor has the right to the goods purchased upon default and within a certain time frame; seek legal advice for current rules. Most credit cards can be obtained by mail or at a retail store location. You may get guaranteed offers or simply offers to apply through the mail (ITA); make sure you read the information packages they come with to ensure full knowledge of the services they will provide and the fees they will charge. They all come with their own credit card agreement; normally a summarized agreement is attached to the application. As with anything, it is a good idea to read the agreement before you sign or send the application for processing. There may be terms such as adjustable rates, introductory rates, balloons, or calls. They may also charge you an initial fee or an annual fee, and you should be aware of the future terms and fees. Shopping around for the right credit card with the right options is a good idea. We have dedicated another section to describing the various types of interest plans and how they can charge the consumer; for terms you do not understand it is familiarly simple to look these up on line.

In many cases you can authorize someone to use your credit card account, such as a son or daughter. An authorized user is typically not responsible for repayment of the debt yet can purchase and use the credit card the same as the responsible party would. So be sure you know the intent of the authorized user before you assign them that authority. Some credit card companies will report the card holder and the authorized user to the credit bureau reporting agencies but under different types of usages or responsibility. All credit cards can be cancelled, so make sure you follow the correct procedure as outlined in their agreement to ensure you actually cancel the card when that is your intention. Many financial institutions now offer cash advances at automatic teller machines (ATMs) as part of their services, so be aware that the authorized user can do this as well; typically there is a personal identification number that they would need to know in order to use it at an ATM, though.

Most credit cards have a particular interest rate assigned to purchases versus cash advances. Be aware of the terms as you use your credit card. In addition, many Visa, and MasterCard issuers also send real checks to your home that you can use as cash advances. Be careful with these checks: Shred them if you don't intend to use them, as they can be used in a fraud scheme and may cost you, at a minimum, time to correct and a maximum of their value (the purchases or cash advances) if you do not provide proof you did not use them. Again read those offers carefully to ensure that you understand the terms of the agreement.

Credit cards often have different interest terms and are really the most expensive form of borrowing for the consumer, so be aware of the transactions you enter into.

Section 1 Credit Options
Chapter 2:

Types of Interest and Loan Terms

As always make sure you know what you are signing and what the documents tell you. We dedicate a chapter to all types of documents and fees later in the book. We will also discuss the different types of loans and how they are closed and the various types of lenders.

There are many ways to charge interest and a variety of terms (the length of the contract) available on the various types of loans.

Types of Interest

Fixed-rate loans are typically known as the industry standard. All fixed rate means is that the financial institution will charge you a fixed interest rate that is agreed-upon at the onset of the loan for an agreed upon amount of time (term). However, even within the fixed-rate loans, there are terms that the average consumer must watch for. You need to be aware of the fees they will charge and whether they all make sense; if not, ask the financial representative to explain them to you. If after you receive an explanation you still don't understand or if you feel you should not be charged for something, then object; after all, in the end it is your money to repay. Within fixed-rate loans there are also different ways to charge interest. A list of some that are available includes schedule-to-schedule, simple interest, which can be figured in many ways, mainly based on an average daily balance or a monthly average calculation, the rule of 78s, pre-computed interest, and compounded interest. We will cover all these later in this chapter. There are undoubtedly other types, but knowing these common ones will assist you if you encounter one not explained in the book.

Adjustable-rate loans have several types as well. An adjustable rate is one where the interest changes during the contract time frame. Typically adjustable-rate loans start with a lower rate, and after a predetermined time frame the interest rate will be reviewed against the terms called for within the contract and adjusted. These agreements typically have a lower rate to begin with and a certain margin established for the latter rates. A margin is the amount the interest rate will be increased over a predetermined index. An index is a base that the financial institution chooses to use, such as T-bills, for determining the interest of your loan. Libor is a common index; be careful of the index as it could be a highly flexible one and therefore cause trouble with your making your monthly payment. There are standard contracts that would have a fixed interest for the first two to three years and then adjust based upon an index. There are also introductory-rate loans, where the loan will start at a certain rate, also unknown as a teaser rate, and at a predetermined time, such as twelve (12) months later, the rate will adjust to another interest rate. In some cases it may change to a new "fixed rate" or become adjustable based on other predetermined terms. For example, the loan may start at 6 percent and then in 12 months the contract states that the rate will be adjusted to 4 percent (margin) over the U.S. Treasury interest rate. Now let's assume that the U.S. Treasury interest rate is 10 percent. After this 12-month time frame, the new interest rate would be 14 percent, since the margin is 4 percent. The 10 percent U.S. Treasury interest rate is the index, or the base to which they add the margin, in this case the 4 percent, in order to determine the new adjusted interest rate. The U.S. Treasury is only one index; another one is the Libor rate index. There are many more, so make sure you read all adjustable-rate programs and research the index they intend to use to determine how much the interest rates might fluctuate within a certain time period so you know how your loan with react. When deciding on an adjustable-rate loan versus a fixed-rate loan you must be prepared for the worst. Within many adjustable-rate contracts they establish a floor and a ceiling, which means that the rate will not go below or above a certain percentage amount.

Features Used on Different Types of Loans

If in fact you will be receiving a fixed-rate loan with no other "terms" that would adjust the loan and the loan doesn't have any other clauses and is strictly fixed, then the only features you need to be aware of are the terms with which they intend to calculate your interest. Some fixed-rate loans have a call or a balloon; we will discuss that in a moment. We will cover interest calculations later; for now let's discuss adjustable-rate loan features.

Adjustable-rate loans have several other features to be aware of. There are caps, also unknown as ceilings, which is typically the most an interest rate can be increased to. For example, if you start your loan at 5 percent and they establish a cap of 10 percent, then your interest will never go above 10 percent no matter what the market does; again be careful of the wording within the contract to ensure that it doesn't say something beyond that. There are floors, which are predetermined interest rates that the loan will not go below. For example you might start your loan at 5 percent, and let's assume the financial institution has set the floor at 5 percent; then it will not go below that. The caps are set in order to protect the consumer from trying to pay a loan they cannot afford, so that the interest rate doesn't go beyond what they can afford to repay. The floors are set to protect the financial institution from having an unprofitable loan due to interest rates dropping below profitability. Adjustable-rate loans add risk to the consumer and take some of the future risk that a financial institution might have to take on if the loan were fixed and the interest rates dropped dramatically. Adjustment periods are predetermined at the onset of the contract. Typically interest rates are reviewed either quarterly or annually; review the contract to determine how often the interest may change. The actual adjustment period is the time frame when the interest rate can adjust based on the index and the margin as described earlier. So the index will be reviewed and the margin will be taken into account and the interest rate for the loan may then be adjusted to the newly calculated rate during the adjustment period. This adjustment, up or down, will typically have an effect upon your monthly payment, which is what you must be prepared for.

Other features to be aware of for adjustable-rate loans are that they may have balloon payments or calls. A balloon payment is the amount you still owe once you have completed the pre-set length of time the loan is taken out for, also known as the term, or number of years the loan will be taken out for. Calls are basically the same; it is the time when the lender can say that you need to pay the loan in full. Balloon payment amounts are normally predetermined based on the amount of time you take the loan out for and assumes you will make payments as described in your agreement and on time. If you pay more than you agreed to pay monthly you can reduce the balloon payment, which typically comes at the end of your contract. A call is the time frame within which the lender says you must close out the loan, or pay it off. This call period could mean that you must refinance, but you don't have to with the same lender. Calls and balloons are risky for the consumer; they may lead to financial difficultly in the future if and when the payment adjusts to a higher level than the consumer can afford. Many lenders have this terminology in their contracts, but not all lenders enforce the call time frame. With the marketplace being so competitive, lenders do not want to lose customers. Balloons once established are not optional for the financial institution, as the amount must be paid when the time comes to have the contract paid as agreed. There normally is not a certain amount that they have predetermined with the call; only the time frame. Balloon payments and calls are typically used with adjustable-rate loans, but can be used with fixed-rate, closed-end loans, so again make sure you read the agreement to determine if you have a balloon or call. In addition, you always have the right to ask the lender, closer, or attorney about any terms within a contract that you do not understand. If you are unable to refinance or pay off the debt upon the balloon payment due date or call date you could risk foreclosure.

Different Types of Loans

With closed-end loans you could have adjustable or fixed interest rate plans. Closed end means that once you have taken out the loan you cannot borrow against the loan without refinancing. Closed end also means that there is a preset time frame in which you are to repay the debt within. For example, let's say you are taking out a car loan and they say what term would you like, five or seven years? The five or seven years are the terms of the loan or the repayment periods. The term is the number of years you have to pay off the debt and the basis on which the financial institution will calculate your monthly payments. Closed-end loans typically have a preset amortization schedule. An amortization schedule simply means the schedule that you use to determine the amount you would need to pay monthly in order to pay off the debt within the repayment time frame. For example, if you set up the loan to be repaid within 15 years, then you would calculate the monthly payment based on that time frame, and a list of the monthly payments you would pay and the balance afterwards, listed by month and or year, would be your amortization schedule.

With revolving loans you normally have a credit limit against which you can continuously borrow throughout the term of the loan. In many cases they will set up an amortization schedule for the revolving loan but not set up a call time. What that means is that the lender will expect you to repay a certain payment monthly, but in many cases they are aware that you will not pay off the debt within a scheduled term. As you can imagine, if you continue to borrow against the credit limit you will not pay off the debt within the original amortization schedule; your payment will continue to adjust based on your usage. In addition, many lenders do not require you to make monthly payments that would ensure you pay off by a certain date. Some financial institutions only require you to pay the interest they have earned or in some case a certain percent of the balance. This practice does cost the consumer a lot of money in finance charges, so be careful of these types of indebtedness.

As you might imagine, if a closed-end or revolving loan is set up with an adjustable rate, the amortization schedule is only a picture in time. Since there is no true prediction of exactly how your rate will alter, then there cannot be a true and exact amortization of your loan based on an adjustable rate. The same holds true if you do not make your payments as agreed; then your amortization schedule will not hold true. This works both ways: If you make your payments late then you will not pay off the loan as agreed or according to the amortization schedule. However, if you pay extra you should be able to pay the loan off early; how early depends on how they calculate interest and how much extra you pay. Please review the calculate interest section. Please recognize that when you pay the minimums on your credit cards you will not pay off the credit and will pay extra interest to the lender; overall it is not best to just pay the minimums.

Terms for Loans

How much you borrow and the type of account you obtain will determine the variety of terms that are available to you. Typically, personal loans, auto loans, and credit cards have shorter terms, such as one year to seven years. The reason they keep these loans on a shorter term is because the amount you typically borrow on a personal basis is lower than you would with a mortgage. In addition, these types of loans are riskier than a mortgage would be, and therefore financial institutions would prefer to maintain these receivables as short term. Additionally, let's say you have an auto loan; that security isn't worth as much after a certain time, which is why they limit the terms for those loans as well. Mortgages normally carry terms such as 5 years through 30 years; within the past couple of years they have come out with 40- to 50-year loans. These terms only distort your viewpoint of the monthly payment and how much you can afford. A 40- or 50-year loan is not as reasonable for the average consumer. As we discussed earlier, you can also have an adjustable rate, which might have a two- to three-year fixed option with a 28- to 27-year adjustable period, which would amount to a 30-year loan, but under different terms during time periods within the life cycle of the loan. You could also have a 15-year term with a balloon that is amortized over a 30-year term. What that means is you have to pay the loan off in 15 years, and yet the monthly payments will be figured upon a 30-year repayment term, which means the payments will be lower but you would pay very little to principal and end up with a fairly large balloon payment. Another thing to consider when you are choosing how long you would like your loan to be for is the amount of interest that the financial institution earns during your chosen term. For example, if you borrow $1,000, you don't want to extend that loan to three year because you would pay so much more in interest versus a one-year term. Another thing you can do is to take the loan for a longer term than you intend to keep the loan out for and make additional payment to pay off early. Since you do not have to pay this extra, if you come upon hard times you wouldn't be tied to the larger payment.

Examples:

If you take out $1,000 over a one-year term at 10 percent interest rate it will cost $87.92 monthly. So to get your annual payments, you calculate $87.92 x 12 (months) = $1055.04; the financial institution will earn 55.04 in one year. If you take that same $1,000 and make the term two years at the same 10 percent interest rate, the payment would only be

$46.14 monthly. Calculating the annual payment, $46.14 X 24 (months) = 1107.36, you can see that you pay almost double in interest. Now let's take a much larger dollar amount for an example and you will see why term is important to consider. Say you take out a $100,000 mortgage for 15 years and let's say the interest rate will be 6 percent; the monthly payments should be $843.86. Now multiply that $843.86 X 180 (15 years x 12 months = 180 months) = $151,894.80, so the institution makes $51,894.80 in interest for the 15-year term. The annual amount they earn is $3459.65. Now let's take our same example and use a 20-year term, which is 240 months. The monthly payments should be $716.43, multiplied by 240 = $171,943.20, which means that the institution will earn $71,943.20, or $3,497.16 per year for 20 years. One more, same example except for 30 years (which is 360 months): The monthly payments should be $599.55 multiplied by 360 = $215,838.00, which means the institution makes $115,838.00 for the 30 years, or $3861.27 per year. So as you can see the lower monthly payment is a benefit, but it must be considered against the interest you will pay. These calculations are based on a real estate calculator so may not be exact for the smaller loan example above. You can figure monthly payments and how much interest you will pay yourself, but you must make sure you have the right type of calculator; you cannot just multiply the term by the balance and have your answer. The right type of calculator will typically have some notation about "real estate" calculator and will have buttons on it that would represent the amount, payment, term, and interest (rate). If you are unsure about your purchase ask a sales person to explain. There are also monthly calculations on the Internet you might what to research. Most calculators have books with them to explain how to calculate these items. You could also read the box to ensure that the calculations you would like to master are simple; many calculators do not make it as easy as others.

A couple of other things to watch for: A recapture clause within a contract typically permits the lender the right to retake the money lent, under certain conditions. Since this is typically not used in an average financial transaction we will not go beyond that for a definition; if you encounter that clause it should tell under what conditions and such. In addition, you always have the right to ask the lender, closer, or attorney about any terms within a contract.

Another thing to watch for is a prepayment penalty clause. In essence this is a fee that the lender will charge if you pay off the loan before the prepayment penalty period ends. So if you intend to only borrow the money for a short time you should not elect a loan with a prepayment clause. However, if the financial institution offers a lower rate or other more favorable terms if you elect the prepayment penalty, it may make sense for your situation. Remember that refinancing a loan into another loan will result in payoff the original loan, and therefore the prepayment penalty would apply. There are lenders that allow you to refinance with them and they would not charge you that fee, but you must at least watch for this.

Different Ways to Calculate Interest

There are many ways in which financial institutions calculate interest. We will outline many here, but there are others. If you come across one not described here make sure you research it and maybe even consult a financial advisor. In many cases we will try to simplify your understanding of the concept; further explanations can be found with additional research.

As described previously, there are fixed-rate loans and adjustable-rate loans, and both can be figured in many different ways. Most mortgage loans are calculated on what is called a schedule-to-schedule basis. All that means is that the amortization is preset based upon the borrower making the monthly payments on time and within the term that was chosen at the onset of the loan. On this basis, if you make your payments late you will still be charged the same amount of interest for that month as it is already figured; however, you may incur *other* fees, such as a late charge. Keep in mind that this does not mean that you shouldn't make your monthly payments on time—whenever possible you should pay on time—this is just an explanation of how the interest for a month is calculated based on the schedule-to-schedule method. Another option mortgage lenders use is simple interest, which can be figured in more than one way. You can figure the simple interest loan based on an average daily balance, which means that you calculate what the average balance is for any given month and then multiply that by the number of days in that month and by the interest rate to calculate the interest. Then you determine what the average is, take what the balance is on each day of the previous month, which adds interest earned once on a specific date, usually the same day you calculate the average daily balance, possibly insurance costs earned, and possibly other fees; then you would need to consider any additional purchases (if that option is available on that type of account) and any payments made during the month. Once you have the average daily balance you can then calculate the interest for that loan based on the interest rate you have contracted. The majority of credit card companies charge interest based on this theory, and you can typically find an explanation on the back of your credit card statement. Financial institutions can also determine the interest they earn based on a compounded interest basis. This type is usually used for credit cards but could also be on other types of loans. When a company charges interest in a compound nature they are essentially charging interest on the interest they earned during the same period in order to calculate the interest they earned for that entire time period. For example, if a credit card is trying to determine the average daily balance, and they intend to compound the interest, they determine what the balance was on each day and add the interest that they earned that day to the balance before they consider it the balance for the day to be added to the averaging. The term simple interest can be misunderstood as well; you can have a simple interest loan that has pre-computed interest (or pre-determined interest). However, pre-computed loans are normally for auto, boat, and personal use loans and typically not mortgages. In fact, many states prohibit financial institutions from charging pre-computed interest altogether, and some prohibit this practice for only the real estate loans. Pre-computed interest is typically described as interest that is calculated at the onset of the loan based on the amount you intend to borrow, at what interest rate, and for how long. So then they would add the interest onto this loan amount to come up with a total repayable amount. For example, if you intend to borrow $10,000 and you want to take this loan out for 10 years and the interest rate will be 10 percent, your monthly payments would be $132.15, with a total repayable amount of $23,787.13. Of the $23,787.13, $13,787.13 would be the pre-computed interest. Based upon the borrower paying the debt back as agreed, this is the amount he/she would pay. As an additional method of calculation, an institution is allowed to use the rule of 78s in order to determine the amount of unearned interest if the borrower pays the loan off early. In most cases, if you pay off a pre-computed loan within the first year or so you benefit, but once you are well into the contract the financial institution has earned most of its interest. There are probably entire books written on the rule of 78, so we will just summarize. In summary, using the rule of 78 the lender earns approximately two-thirds of the interest within the first one-third of the contract.

Repayment Options

There are many ways to repay the different types of credit. Let's first discuss in an overview forum, and then we can provide you with options. The goal is to reduce the amount of interest you will pay on any loans, minimize the additional fees you may have to pay, and maintain your credit in good standing.

Let's discuss briefly how payment options help for different types of accounts. When you pay off your credit cards monthly, when you receive the bill, most of the time you will eliminate the interest charges. Although some credit cards do charge interest for the first 30 days, most do not, and in fact that is something to look for when deciding which credit card to use. Many credit cards also offer same-as-cash options, such as 90 days, 6 months, and 12 months. Typically these offers apply to a certain purchase at a certain store. If you have this type of option you should take advantage of it and only pay the minimum they ask for until it is time to pay it off. In some cases it will be deferred, which just means you don't pay until that 90 days, 6 months, or 12 months is up. If you have one of these options be careful that you do in fact pay it off one time, at least a day or two early, unless you are mailing and then allow for that time frame. Once the time period expires, in many cases the lender will have the right to charge you all the way back to the beginning if you do not pay off on time, and paying it partially will not negate this. As we discussed earlier, there are credit offers out there that offer an introductory-rate option, if you have acquired one of these, obviously use it to your advantage and pay off more expensive debts during that period while allowing the lower interest rate accounts to only be maintained with minimum monthly payments. If you are being proactive to pay off all your debt by a certain time, then a budget that you establish to do just that should be created. We have a chapter on budgets later.

No matter what type of debt you have, paying it off early, if for no other reason, may provide peace of mind. You have many options available to you. Try to consider using the financial institution's money wisely. If you are presented with a weekly, biweekly, or a semi-monthly option, you should ask the representative about those options and how exactly they help you versus the standard monthly payment. In many cases it can at least help you budget to pay off debt faster, or it can even reduce the amount of interest you will pay. For example, if you have a simple interest loan and the interest is calculated using the average daily balance method, then you could benefit from paying weekly, biweekly or semi-monthly, because you would pay extra on the principal while the lender would only have earned a portion of their interest. For simple interest rate loans these methods would provide the most benefit. For example, if you were paying weekly, then you would be posting payments every seven days, which means they would only earn seven days worth of interest at a time, and when they calculate their interest earned they will take into account the fact that you paid on principal during the month. In addition to that you would make extra payments per year (assuming you continue with the weekly payments for the entire year), since there are 52 weeks in a year and only 12 months (times 4 would be 48); so you would actually make one additional monthly payment per year. As we discussed earlier you can use a financial calculator to determine payments; most of them will also tell you the savings you will recap if you pay in these smaller increments. When you enter into one of these types of payment plans, make sure you keep up as agreed, or the adverse could happen—you could end up paying more interest; in many cases this is considered an interest short situation. Simple interest loans are great for people who can keep up an extra payment plan, but not so good for someone who can only pay sporadically. With a schedule-to-schedule loan the extra amount of payments you would be making would be what provides you with the benefits, not the savings of interest. The savings will vary based on how they calculate their interest; you will save more with a simple interest loan if you pay extra than with a schedule-to-schedule loan, and those features cannot be altered once you enter into the loan, so ask questions about their interest options prior to taking out the loan.

An additional payment tool to use is online banking, automatic withdrawal, or a one-time debt. Online banking helps you keep in touch with your information, but if you are not familiar with the programs and online systems, you could potentially cause yourself trouble. There are some very simple software programs that can assist you in becoming familiar with the online functions and allow you to use these methods with ease. You can set up your payments to come out of a checking or savings account on a weekly, biweekly, or monthly basis—although some financial institutions only offer monthly. If you set up this type of payment option, make sure you set it up for a time frame such that you will always have the funds available for disbursements. If you don't have the money you may be charged by both the lender and the bank for an overdraft and nonsufficient funds; these can add up and be very expensive. Many lenders offer an interest rate discount if you set up your payments on the automatic basis, but make sure you can meet those dates, as the interest savings will not cover the overdraft charges, and in some case the overdraft will cause your bank to close your account. Many institutions charge exorbitant fees to set you up with this program; this services should not cost a lot. Be cautious about whom you give your banking account information to and be aware of the lender's right to access the same. If you are in collections they may use that information against you to attach liens to those known accounts.

In many cases lenders will offer you a deferred interest payment, a skip a payment option, or a reschedule or restructure-modification. These options differ from lender to lender, so you will need to review the offer carefully before you agree to it. A deferred interest payment usually means that the lender is offering to place your monthly payment at the end of your loan and accept an interest-only amount for a predetermined time period. A skip a payment is essentially the same thing except they do not collect the interest amount; instead they place the entire payment at the end of the contract. The deferred interest payment is typically used to help someone through a difficult time or a seasonal need, while the skip a payment is usually used as a marketing tool to provide a thank you to good-paying customers. A reschedule, restructure, or a modification agreement can be used during hard times to assist consumers in getting back on their feet; depending upon the agreement, it may be a practical option, especially if you are nearly or in foreclosure, when you may be able to negotiate a forbearance agreement. If the lender has offered to bring your account current under this agreement and allow you to pay the past due amount at the end of the contract instead of requiring you to pay the account up to date right away, you might benefit; at least review the terms of the agreement.

If you have come upon difficult times you may even want to consider a nonprofit credit counselor. Many of these programs are offered through nonprofit companies and basically have employees who will work with the creditors to reduce your monthly payments, interest, and fees being charged. Most of them have standing agreements with the larger creditors. Some of these agreements could include a specific interest rate they will lower your rate to during this agreement, or a promise to waive all future late charges. Keep in mind that these programs help you reduce your monthly payments and interest, but they do not improve or maintain your credit in all cases. This credit counselor situation usually establishes a budget that you must follow; you can even be dropped from the plan if you don't keep up with your portion of the agreement. Sometimes it is a choice you have to make, and many creditors even respect someone who goes into a plan and completes it. From a creditor's perspective a credit-counseling situation is better than a bankruptcy, which should only be used in the most extreme situation. If you plan and stick to it there is no reason for that final option—bankruptcy; we will discuss this later, and of course it should only be used as a final resort.

In some cases your hard time may be due to a medical illness. Some creditors offer credit insurance at the onset of the lending process. If you elected that insurance, and you meet the qualifications under the insurance agreement, they may make your monthly payments for you. For disability insurance plans, most credit insurance plans require you to be fully off work for a certain period of time, and a doctor has to sign off that they have authorized you to be off for your illness. These credit insurance plans typically have a certain amount of time to process your claim, so once you are off work you should start looking into this, or someone else that can help you with your finances should. You of course are responsible for your debt even if you have this insurance, so be prepared to pay if there is a delay in processing. For unemployment insurance, most insurance plans only pay for certain things; read your agreement, as your loss of work may not qualify. Make sure that you understand that if you pay this cost of insurance there is only the possibility it would cover you for certain situations and only for the loan you take it out on. Make sure you weigh the costs against the possible future benefits to ensure it is worth it.

Section 2 Maintaining Your Debt
Chapter 1:

Life-Altering Occurrences

Death of a Co-Applicant

In many cases you will not be responsible to pay off your co-applicant's debt upon their death because there hopefully was insurance that will provide coverage to pay it off. You will still be responsible for researching to see if there was coverage and for filing the claim(s). If there was no insurance coverage for the debt, you could be held responsible if you signed the debt with someone that passed on. Additionally you will want to follow up to ensure payment. Insurance companies have a certain amount of time to process any claim, so make sure they received your claim and that they do not need additional information in order to process your claim; that would delay the process. There may also be an estate that will need to be settled, and in the meantime while either the insurance is processing or the estate is being settled you are responsible for the normal monthly payments. You can of course contact each creditor and ask them if they will defer payment or work with you during this time, and many will. You can always fall back on consumer credit counseling for assistance, as discussed earlier.

Medical Issues

As stated in a prior chapter, you are still responsible for the debt even though you may have a medical condition. Make sure you also research to see if you have insurance coverage and that the claim is being processed with all the information that they need and in a timely manner. Once again you can contact the creditors to ask for some concessions.

Divorce

As with any medical situation, if in fact you are cosigned on a loan with someone whom you are now divorcing you are equally responsible for your debts. In many cases this is a difficult situation to go through, because you as a couple are trying to decide how the assets and liabilities will split. To ensure that your credit stays in good standing, you have to make arrangements with the creditors you are unable to pay on your own if your co-applicant does not pay. If your partner states they will pay certain bills, it is to your benefit to follow up with that creditor to make sure your partner did in fact pay, and on time. If you share a credit card or any debt that allows future advances, you do have the right to contact them and refuse to pay further advances; in many cases they will allow you to close out the credit limit altogether. The same conditions apply if you are only separated as well. Your divorce decree should outline who is responsible for what, but keep in mind that your creditors still have the enforceable loan agreement. This loan agreement does not make concessions for divorce, and the creditor maintains the "right" to collect from both parties even if a divorce decree says only one is responsible.

Bankruptcy/Foreclosure

There will be a section later that goes into more detail about bankruptcy and foreclosure.

Repossession

Repossession is normally when a lender takes back property that the borrower pledged for security and proceeds to sell it in order to recover the amount owed. In many cases the lender will not be able to recover the full amount, so even if a consumer allows the creditor to reposs something, it doesn't mean that they are clear of that debt. In many case the lenders has auction houses, bulk buyers already set up, and those parties provide the lender with an immediate sale, but for less money. As with foreclosure you may owe additional funds. This remedy is also costly to the lender and time consuming.

As we enter into the section that discusses budget and exit from the life-altering occurrences, I would like to discuss debt in general. Always be sure you know what type of contract you are entering into and signing, and try to be prepared for events that we hope will not happen and only borrow within your means. Means is a broad term, but if you do not have stable employment, then that isn't part of your means. If you occasionally have a part-time job, don't include that in your available monthly income. Try to put away some money into a savings account so that if something happens you can at least sustain while you refinance or consolidate your debt to get you through this tough time.

Let's talk for a moment about checking and saving accounts. You should establish a checking account and a savings account. Most employers allow you to direct deposit your income, which makes it available sooner. A checking account can help you to realize how much to spend or not to spend. You must recognize that only if you have the money in your checking account can you use that money to pay a bill or purchase something. Once a check has been deposited into your checking account you must allow the funds to become available. If your employer allows you to direct deposit you should elect to deposit some of your funds into a savings account. Even if there is a possibility that you would withdraw those funds later you might be able to save more. It is easier to spend the money from your checking account than it is to have to withdraw it from your savings in order to spend it. A savings account is very important for those times when you need funds that you didn't realize you would need. Let's say your car breaks down and you can't afford to just pay for it; then you can turn to your savings for the money.

Budget Planning

<u>What Is a Debt Ratio?</u>

A debt ratio is a mathematical equation where you add all of your monthly income up and consider that to be your incoming funds. Then you add all of your monthly liabilities up and consider that to be your outgoing funds. You then take your incoming and divide it by your outgoing to arrive at your debt to income ratio. For example, if your monthly income from your full-time job is $3,000, and you have rental income of $700 a month, and your spouse has a part-time job making $500 a month, then you would add those three to arrive at your income of $4,200.00 a month. Then let's say that you have the following debts: mortgage payment of $750, auto payment of $350, credit card debts of $150 a month on average; then you would have a total of $1,250.00 a month in monthly outgoing. So you would take the $4200.00 and divide that by the $1,250 and you would have approximately a 30 percent debt to income ratio. Now let's keep in mind that we have only done this calculation based on a gross income factor and only consider the monthly bills that are actually debts. You have taxes, health insurance, and any other work-related deductions that we did not consider, plus you have monthly utilities, gas, food, and entertainment. Generally speaking, a gross debt to income ratio of 30 percent is good. Many financial institutions figure debt to income ratios differently. Some figure it based on gross and net; some consider those additional monthly debts and some do not; and many will consider child support payments, alimony, and pension plans into your debt ratio. The most important thing to consider is that you only finance what you know you can pay monthly; what you can barely pay monthly should not be financed.

Pitfalls

Many times we as individuals will see something that we want and they offer financing. We get approved for this financing and believe that they would not approve us if we could not pay for it, so we purchase it. Many financial institutions lend on credit quality alone; if the amount is small enough according to their guidelines and your credit is in good standing you end up with a loan you truly cannot afford. Some auto finance transactions are approved based on the fact that the debt will be secured and the person has adequate credit to justify the transaction. Another thing to consider is that there are always things that come up, whether it is you need new tires for your used vehicle or your daughter is away at school and needs a loan. You need to consider the possibility of not having the same or as much cash flow every month.

A budget is a good plan, but if you are unable to plan in such detail, then generally keep in mind that you should not borrow so much that you live from paycheck to paycheck. Some warning signs that you are overextended might be: You pay off one credit card with another frequently, you only pay the minimums on your credit cards, you take advances against one credit card to pay bills during a month, and you charge everything you purchase. Some of these warning signs could be

OK if you are taking advances because you received a lower rate offer on another credit card and all you are doing is advancing to take advantage of that offer.

Using Your Home to Consolidate Your Debt

As stated previously, you should plan for the unexpected, but if for some reason you lose a part-time job, your rental property has serious damage and the tenants moved out suddenly (obviously you cannot re-rent it right away), or you have some other occurrence that reduces your monthly income on a fairly permanent basis, then you may need to readjust your debts versus liabilities by considering refinancing your home and consolidating your debt. If your first mortgage was taken out when interest rate were similar to today's rate, then you could consider a full refinance and incorporate the debt consolidation. But if you acquired your loan when interest rates were much lower, then maybe all you need is a second mortgage to consolidate. Never let someone tell you that you must refinance your first mortgage to qualify for a loan, if you feel that is not what you want to do; it is your home and your choice. If the amount of money they will lend you is the same, you should ask why you have to pay off your first mortgage, especially if your interest rate is much lower or you have had the loan opened for a reasonable amount of time so that refinancing it doesn't make sense. Now there may be a situation where the loan is only approved to refinance in entirety because they can carry the entire loan to 30 years and the second mortgage is at a much higher interest rate and they can only lend up to 15 years per their guidelines. In this situation there is a choice to be made. Consider your future and where you want to be and whether refinancing right now will benefit you in the long run. The goal is always to pay off your debt, but consider your options, since sometimes to pay things off you must consolidate them. Review your credit card statements; are you really going to pay them off soon? Past performance is a good indicator of future results. If the total consolidation will benefit you in the long run and you can still meet your goal of paying off everything then it might be right for you. One thing to watch for, though: Once you consolidate and pay off all your additional debt and combine everything into the one mortgage payment, DO NOT go back out and charge your credit cards up again. Keep one in your freezer, frozen in a bucket of water; that means in order to use it you must wait a short time anyway, and therefore it should be an emergency or at least a planned use.

Creating an Actual Budget

Before you start to create your budget, have your mind set that you will plan it and stick to it. A budget is a good idea for everyone, even if you have plenty of money to make your monthly obligations with. Decide what it is you are going to budget for: You have a 15-year plan to eliminate your debts; you want to set aside money for a special family vacation or to build up a college fund for one of your children. Whatever it is, make sure you have it set in your mind prior to the actual budget planning. Now what?

List all of your monthly sources of income and outline the gross and the net income from each, and be conservative.

List all of your monthly expenses. Take some time with this one; you may even have a bill you only pay every other month, such as a waste-management bill. You want to list them all, even if you only pay them quarterly. You can always divide it up so that the monthly budget still makes sense.

Here is an example:

For this example I tried to compile many different types of debt, with no business names. As you can see they save a good amount of money monthly, they have two auto payments, and they pay a good amount into their pension monthly. So if this couple were to have hard times, as you can see, there are many places they could cut back. They could reduce the amount they spend on food, they could reduce their savings or even take from their savings if it is a serious emergency, they could cancel cable, lower their church donations, or eliminate the Internet during this difficult time. Many options are available to them, and having a budget laid out as such allows them to see that. As information, using only the actual debts, this couple has a 29 percent debt ratio.

Now the idea will be to only spend the amounts they have allotted for in each section. So you must write down a budget and track it to be sure you are sticking to it. You may also need to adjust it in some places. Maybe you have found that you need more money for gas; you can take from something else or have less left over money each month, but adjust what you are tracking and continue to track your budget even after adjustments. If you don't watch what you spend and make sure you are in line with your budget you will not feel the need to adhere to it.

Type of Income	Gross Monthly Income	Net Monthly Income
Full-time job (Sue)	$3,000.00	$2,250.00
Full-time job (Sam)	$5,000.00	$3,750.00
Total	$8,000.00	$6,000.00

Type of Expense	Monthly Expenses	Balance
Mortgage Payment (30 yr)	$1,199.00	$200,000.00
T&I (Taxes and Insurance)	$292.00	
Sue's Auto Payment	$220.00	$4,000.00
Auto Insurance	$45.00	
Sam's Auto Payment	$350.00	$6,000.00
Auto Insurance	$65.00	
Visa Payment	$50.00	$5,000.00
MasterCard Payment	$100.00	$2,000.00
Power Bill	$150.00	
Phone Bill	$80.00	
Gas Bill House (pd every other month; calculated for monthly)	$100.00	
Cell Phones	$100.00	
Cable Bill	$50.00	
Internet Bill	$30.00	
Church Donation	$100.00	
Other Credit Cards	$200.00	$6,000.00
Waste Management (Garbage)	$35.00	
Kids' Lunches	$110.00	
Exercise Place	$50.00	
Food	$800.00	
Auto Gas	$173.00	
Life Insurances	$100.00	
Pension Funds	$800.00	
Health Insurance	$60.00	
Monthly Savings	$500.00	
Extra Funds	$241.00	
	$6,000.00	$223,000.00

Section 2 Maintaining Your Debt
Chapter 2:

How Do Credit Bureau reports Work?

This is a very popular question now that the word is out: Your credit bureau report has a scoring that affects your ability to obtain credit. One other thing to consider is that most financial institutions also use an internal scoring as well as a credit bureau agency scoring system. In addition to that many also have the credit bureau agencies provide them with a risk score based on the information in the credit bureau report (CBR). Sometimes the financial institution will get the same information from three credit sources and take the middle one. There is no way to know what the makeup of every score is, but there are some basic guidelines to follow to ensure you have a decent score. We will discuss what is on your report and tips to use in maintaining yours.

What Is on the Credit Report?

Normally the credit bureau agencies will have your basic information such as name, social security number, date of birth, most recent address known, most recent employer known, and sometimes your former address and employer. They will have credit accounts, including all credit cards, auto loans, personal loans, student loans, and mortgages in your name, with information about the creditor and a partial account number, last reported balance, date opened, payment history, with a current status, recent credit inquiries (other services could inquire as well, such as employer, insurance company etc.), and any accounts that are in collections. They will also have a section on judgments, open or paid status, when opened, and the amount. If you have a judgment and it is released later that may show up as well. This section could also have civil judgments, bankruptcies, foreclosure information, and tax liens. Most credit reports have a seven-year history from the date last paid on the account and retain the judgment section for 10 years. The credit bureau agencies report information given to them through various sources; as the creditors, court reporting, and such. There are rules around what can be reported and for how long. You also have the right to dispute items you find on your credit report that you disagree with.

Credit Scoring

As we discussed, there are credit bureau agency scores and there are lenders scores. It isn't important to know exactly what the scores are made of, but it is useful to know generally what they look at so that you can maintain a good score. Credit bureau agencies obviously use credit information such as how many accounts you have, how recently you have opened them, do you have them charged up to the limit, total amount of debt, how you are paying your debt (on time or not), and how many credit inquiries you have had. In many cases they will consider bad debt that is old even if you have a good history currently; it will still be counted in the scoring but not weighted as heavily. They will also consider the same for your recently opened accounts and credit inquiries. If you have opened a lot of debt recently or have had a lot of credit inquiries it is given a negative look; the overall rating may be just fine depending on how much of what kind of debt you have. Things to try and maintain your score might be to only let a creditor inquiry into your credit report if you are sure you want the account, and to make sure you don't open various different accounts all at once. Also make sure you maintain your credit with a good monthly payment history and do not have the credit cards charged up to the limit. Even medical bills and utilities can report if you don't pay them they will report to the credit bureau agenecies as collections, which is not good. These are just a few tips to consider. You could do additional research, but be careful, as many of the web sites are trying to sell you a score versus educate you about it. Typically, if you are ever turned down for a loan you have the right to inquiry with the credit bureau agency that they used to obtain a credit bureau report, usually free of charge; in doing so you can hopefully see the areas that need correcting and make adjustments to get it corrected. There is recent regulation that allows you to have one free credit bureau report per year and to have a disclosure of your score from creditors that you apply with.

Credit BureauReports and Co-applicants

As stated earlier if you are a co-applicant it is likely that credit you have established with someone else will also report to your credit bureau. Even if you do not have the responsibility to pay it, if you are an authorized user, in many cases it reports to your bureau. So as stated earlier make sure when you enter into these contracts you are certain of the other person's ability and character to pay.

Other Things that Affect a Credit Bureau Report

We already discussed bankruptcy as a last resort, and credit reports make it even more important, as they maintain that information for 10 years. In many cases it isn't just a one-line bankruptcy note; it is all the creditors' ratings that you let them charge off, and then the bankruptcy dates, discharge, and type are noted. If you have filed several bankruptcies, they will show up until each is 10 years old, so it is possible to have more than one on a credit bureau report at a time—not a good view from a lender's point of view. Even if you file and later decide not to complete the process it will show up as a dismissal. These will also seriously affect your credit bureau score. We also talked about consumer credit counseling. While this is a good program to help you get out of debt and improve your future ability to borrow and maintain your credit, in the short term it may affect your credit bureau report. Some creditors will restructure your account so that it reports current, but others do not. In a case where they don't, the rating will likely show that you are not paying as agreed, as you are not; you are likely paying less per month. Rest assured that if you get through the plan it won't matter as you will have accomplished a complete cleanup and you can rebuild from there. No creditor likes to say that they consider certain bad debts worse than other, but the fact is that the computer might not, but the person will. Most financial institutions still have some sort of manual underwriting process, even if it is just for re-look situations. A re-look would typically be a loan for which the guidelines did not allow an automatic approval to go through, or somehow the computer noted that this loan should be reviewed manually for some reason. So what order of importance is there? This will not be exact or apply to all institutions, and likely it will depend on what type of credit you are applying for. Typically the most important would be mortgages and then auto loans, personal loans, and then credit cards. However, if you have a history of not paying your credit cards on time and you are applying for a credit card, they will be looking closely at your credit card history.

State and Federal Agencies

Every state has an attorney general who is very interested in the laws and regulations being followed. If you have a dispute, you could start with the better business bureau, but they are not responsible for making sure that the companies comply with the laws; they are there to note the complaints and try to get them resolved. In many cases you can get a dispute resolved through them, but if the dispute is of a serious nature the attorney general will listen, and if you should go elsewhere for your dispute they will advise you. As far as federal agencies, for the regulations that we will discuss later there are many agencies in charge of monitoring for compliance. I found a decent web site for searching where to complain:

http://mortgage-x.com/general/federal.htmlsts

Community Activist Groups

There are too many community activist groups to be familiar with all of them, but like with anything else, there is a side for and a side against them. The activist groups typically represent people who don't understand contracts, agreements, and such, and they try to assist the consumer in ways they know others have had difficulties. Large corporations today cannot afford reputation risk, so these groups have the power to get these companies to at least listen to a consumer's concerns. This of course is an alternative way to initiate a complaint. One well known group for the financial industry is Acorn. They have been fairly active in the last couple of years.

Class-Action Lawsuits and Settlements

In the twenty-first century there has been an increase in the amount of concern about what financial institutions have been doing and what they should be doing. If you haven't already heard about it there was a law put into place to try and outline what is not acceptable sales behavior (UDAP). This is outlined in the regulations section for further explanations. In addition to the sales practices concern, there has been a heightened awareness of some of the older laws that institutions have become more relaxed with over the years.

A class-action lawsuit normally involves as many of the possible claimants that the party handling the case is aware of. For example, the anti-money-laundering regulations were put into place prior to the current terrorist activity. Now more than ever banks must make sure to comply with this regulation, and many banks of late have been fined due to the discovery that they are not 100 percent compliant. Most of those fines where purely paid to the government.

You may find yourself in a situation where you are notified of a financial institution that you were involved with that is actually in a lawsuit. In many cases there are third parties that handle the claims. The same holds true for settlements. These settlements and class actions that you obviously did not initiate are normally from a activist or large legal firm seeking to assist the "many" people who are not aware of an issue or who do not have the means to take this type of action against such large companies.

Section 3 Collections
Chapter 1:

Fair Debt Collection Practices (FDCPA)

Generally the FDCPA is an act that was put into effect to protect the consumer from unfair collection practices. Many consumers were complaining about creditors calling them at all hours of the day, several times a day, and other activities like calling their work places that were deemed inappropriate. This act truly only applies to third-party companies that are collecting another institution's debt. However, many large financial institutions train their employees to follow similar rules. One example of a well-known rule is that you can only contact a person once in a day, in some cases less often if it doesn't make sense. For example, if you promised to pay on a certain date then the creditor should not call you until after that date. If a creditor tells a consumer that they will sue them or repossess something that must be their intent—not just to threaten.

Here is a web site that outlines the entire act:

http://www.ftc.gov/os/statutes/fdcpa/fdcpact.htm

Use of Alias Names

An alias is another name for you on your credit report, or maybe you are even using it for credit cards, bank accounts, etc. It may be another name under which you have applied for credit (a nickname, or a variation of your name, for example) or it may be the name of someone else. It is possible, if an alias appears on your credit report, that actual fraud was involved. Someone else may have applied for credit using your qualifications, and the name they used may have been entered as an alias.

If you find an alias on your credit report, and it does not belong to you, contact the credit bureau agency immediately to have it removed.

Automatic Withdrawal Cautions

During the collection process it may seem necessary to pay a bill over the phone by providing your checking or savings information for a one-time withdrawal. Once you have given them your information, there are a few things that might happen. The collections department truly needs your authorization in order to perform this withdrawal, but you might find that a collector uses it and says you advised it was OK. Another thing that might happen is that you gave the information to an institution and then later you become delinquent enough for them to take legal action, in which case they could use that information and give it to their attorney to use for attaching a lien to the accounts in order to recover the money you owe them.

Legal Actions

As you can well imagine, that are many types of legal action. There are entire books written on this subject alone. I would like to highlight some of the more important aspects. If you need further assistance you could research further or obtain legal counsel.

Judgments

A judgment is a court's determination of the rights and obligations of the parties to a case. What does that mean? Well, when you have not paid your creditor(s) for whatever reason, they have the right to take you to court. When you go to court, the judge typically reviews both sides and makes a decision. Keep in mind that if you don't actually go to court the creditor will win by default and the judge does not have your opinion to consider. This decision can be referred to as the judgment order. What the creditor has asked for and whether you have disputed any part of that will determine what the judgment will entail. If the creditor asked for your wages to be garnished and you cannot afford that for some other reason, then it is a very good idea for you to go to court and explain your circumstances to the judge. Judges typically want to make sure a judgment does not harm you further. Once again if you do not show up for court then you will not be afforded this consideration. The judge will have to order by default and allow the creditor their terms requested in the court order.

Attachment of Assets

Now let's talk about the order itself a little further and what some possible outcomes could be. If you have a loan that you did not pay and are far enough behind on it that the creditor has the right to take legal action, then during that court proceeding the creditor could be awarded a lien on your home if that is what the creditor requested and the judge determined that it was a fair and legitimate request under the circumstances. This lien does not "take over" your home but can certainly interfere when you are trying to refinance. You would have to pay off this lien if you were to refinance or want to sell your home. So if you are being sued and you own your home, it is a good idea to go to court and try to work things out; then likely your home would not acquire this attachment. One thing to remember is that this lien is behind whatever you already owe on your home, and it is not likely to be foreclosed upon unless they intend to take on the mortgages you already owe. Another thing worth mentioning is if you have additional properties they can be used for this same purpose. There are many other assets that creditors can legally be granted an attachment to: bank accounts, income wages, rental income, vehicles (boats and motor homes), burial plots, stocks and bonds, stamp collections, coin collections, other hobby collections, certificates of deposit, annuities, and basically any other material thing that has been deemed a valuable asset. Normally your retirement-pension fund is not something the courts allow creditors to attach a lien to, as truly it is a future asset, not really considered a current asset. Make sure you seek legal advice if you have additional assets and you are about to go through some sort of legal action.

Land Trusts

One way to protect your assets from a lawsuit is to enter them into a land trust agreement. Trusts have been used as an entity to hold assets for protection, such as real estate, for many years. As you can imagine, a land trust could also be used to protect large companies, joint ventures, and partnerships. When you enter into a "partnership" your assets are part of the deal unless you protect them. Sometimes people get a land trust when they pass property on to their children so that the children cannot take out liens on the property or lose it in some way. Investors use land trusts to hide their name as an interested party. Land trusts are complicated transactions, and if you intend to enter into one it is not good advice for you to go it alone; you truly need someone you trust to assist you or once again seek legal advice.

Bankruptcy

As stated previously, bankruptcy should be an avenue of last resort. If you become overwhelmed by your monthly debt obligations, calling your creditors and asking them for concessions, restructures, and such should be your first option. Then of course as we discussed you can elect to go with the consumer credit counseling service. Then there is bankruptcy. There are two basic types of bankruptcy for the individual. Chapter 13 is generally considered the type where you create a plan to repay your creditors; sometimes it is all of them and sometimes it is only the secured creditors. Chapter 7 is normally considered a "straight bankruptcy" and is the most common form used. This type of bankruptcy reviews your assets versus your liabilities and then basically gives you allowance for your assets; it will allow you to maintain your secured assets under what is known as a reaffirmation agreement and discharges the rest of your debts. The statements above are only in summary of what bankruptcy is. If you need detailed information, the Internet is a good source for research. Bankruptcy is a federal law; however, many states have different methods/procedures that they require, and if you are considering bankruptcy you should do your research to determine if this is the best option for you and your situation. There is no guarantee that you would be granted a bankruptcy; even if you go through an attorney and they advise that you will, it is possible that the court system could still deny you. These laws were put in place to assist individuals in getting a fresh start, but they have many limitation, requirements, and rules. You must be prepared to follow the "plan" if you decide to file a chapter 13, and if you decide to file chapter 7 you must be prepared to have to sell or give up certain assets. Acquiring an attorney may assist you if you are receiving many collection calls or many creditors have filed lawsuits against you. In many cases the creditors will cease action while you are seeking legal advice about a bankruptcy, but they do not have to stop until you actually file. Even then some creditors could seek relief from the bankruptcy or require payment based on the reaffirmation agreement. A reaffirmation agreement is basically a loan agreement that you enter into during bankruptcy. You typically sign this stating that you will pay a certain amount with monthly payments of a certain amount and at a specific interest rate. Many of these agreements also include provisions for the creditor to be able to establish a claim that you have not followed the agreement. As with any other document, make sure you are aware of what you are signing. Also review the section dedicated to credit bureaus that further explains the effect of bankruptcy on your credit bureau report and future potential lending opportunities.

Foreclosure

Foreclosure is the legal means that your lender can use to repose (take ownership over) your home, also known as the legal process by which an owner's right to a property is terminated, usually due to default. Foreclosure normally only applies to mortgage lending, but as discussed earlier, creditors can be awarded a lien, and if they feel it is worthy they may foreclose on that lien. During the foreclosure process the lender typically forces the sale of the home, and then the home is sold at a public auction and the proceeds are applied to the mortgage balance. When this happens, you must move out of your house. If your property is worth less than the total amount you still owe on your mortgage loan, a deficiency judgment could be pursued. If that happens, you not only lose your home, but you also would owe your lender an additional amount. Foreclosure is a last resort for a lender, much the same as bankruptcy is the last resort for a consumer. Foreclosure costs lenders a lot of money and time. Lenders have to keep up the property during the proceedings if the debtor is not doing the upkeep, such as mowing the lawn, winterizing the property, etc. Foreclosure costs lenders a lot of money and time, and frankly they are not in the business of selling homes, so it isn't what they want to do. Lenders are also not in the business of selling homes, so it isn't what they want to do. They may even offer you a sum of money to avoid foreclosure and work with you on a future move-out date. If by chance you "raise" the money during this process you do have the possibility of retaining your home, but you will need to seek further advice about when that applies.

There are other options as well: If your creditor offers to accept a deed in lieu of foreclosure, you should at least review the proposal with an advisor. These types of agreements usually are just agreements that state that you agree to turn over the home in a certain amount of time and the lender will not hold you accountable further. Some of these agreements may not say they will not hold you accountable further, so make sure you have reviewed the terms of the agreement.

Repossession

Repossession is normally when a lender takes back property that the borrower pledged for security and proceeds to sell it in order to recover the amount owed. Repossession applies to most assets other than a home, and then it has the "foreclosure" name. For some of these items, the creditor will have to go through the court in order to have the right to take the property, but vehicles, for example, can be repossessed without a court case. Once they repose them they need to file some paperwork, but in no way is it as difficult as a foreclosure or legal action. In many cases the lender will not be able to recover the full amount owed, so even if a consumer allows the creditor to repose something, it doesn't mean that they are clear of that debt. In many case the lenders has auction houses and bulk buyers already set up, and those parties provide the lender with an immediate sale, but for less money. As with foreclosure you may owe additional funds. This remedy is also costly to the lender and time consuming.

Co-Applicant Obligations

If you elect to sign a document with someone, you have said you guarantee payment or promise to pay. Now if that debt is not paid, and the applicant has no assets for the creditor to use for recovery purposes, the creditor then has the right to seek your assets. As you have promised as well and you are in default as well, no matter what happened, if you signed the document saying you would pay then you are liable until that debt is paid.

Consolidation of Debts

We have talked about this several times in the book. Many times when you are in a financial struggle your debts should be evaluated. You should determine if the remedies we have discussed are the right ones. Consolidation of your debt may be the right choice. You must be prepared to pay it, though, as normally consolidation means using your home or some other form of security. You should not enter into those transactions lightly; always consider what might happen. If you are consolidating your debts because you are having trouble keeping up on the many payments, and it is because you just got overextended, then you must make sure you plan how you will prevent that from happening again. Charging up credit can be a problem that needs to be thought through. For example, if you have someone who charges everything and they only pay the minimum monthly payment, they are probably living beyond their means. Once this type of problem is identified, then that person must understand that they cannot continue to charge once the debts are consolidated or you will be right back where you started—only worse, since now you probably won't have an asset to use to consolidate with. If you elect to consolidate make sure that the interest you will pay is not more than you are already paying on the debts you are consolidating.

What Debts to Pay First

Of course I would not recommend that you not pay a creditor, as that will only create further problems. But once you have identified a problem and you are trying to solve that problem, or if it is only temporary, like a layoff, then you need to decide what to pay when. The most important bill(s) is you home bill, whether it be rent or mortgage or even association dues. All of those types of payments should be made first. Then you need your vehicle to get to and from work, so that is the next payment. Then you need to consider which other debts are secured and prioritize them according to need. Of course you will need to pay your utilities and such; I am only discussing the actual debts. Many utility companies will also work with you during difficult times and set you up on payment plans like other creditors do so that you can afford to pay other debts.

Section 4
Chapter 1

General Documents

As always make sure you know what you are signing and what the documents tell you.

Security Agreements

All loans have security agreements, even if the security is only your signature. In some cases companies combine the security agreement with the note, also known as a promise to pay. Either way the security agreement typically indicates the terms by which the lender has the rights to the property you pledge for security in order to get a loan. It will normally describe how the lender requires the borrower to carry insurance coverage for the property pledged as security. They do this to ensure that the security is protected and that they will be paid if something happens to it during the loan. Many lenders offer that same type of insurance through the loan, while others require you to list them as a loss payee in the case of a claim. Let's say for example that you have an auto loan and you carried insurance through an insurance company. If you had partial damage and you had to complete repairs and not replace the vehicle, then a check would be issued to you and the lender since you are the owner and they are the loss payee. Once you have the repairs done you will need to provide proof to the lender that their security has been restored, and then they will sign the check over to you so that you can pay the repair shop. Many lenders have verbiage outlining their right to force-place insurance for the property pledged should they receive notice that you are not keeping up with the insurance coverage. This force-placed insurance is typically not of benefit to the consumer; it normally only covers the lender's interest and does not provide replacement. If you receive notification that they intend to force-place insurance, make sure that you respond right away and provide evidence that you have paid your insurance bill. If you change insurance companies, the lender would then receive a notice from the insurance company of cancellation since they are listed as the loss payable. You would then need to make sure you notify them of changes before they occur so that they will not force-place this insurance, and when you change insurance companies make sure the new insurance company lists the lender as the loss payable. If you simply tell the new insurance company that you have a loan for the vehicle, they will know what to do also. Mortgage lenders also have the right to hold the borrower accountable for the insurance coverage and annual real estate taxes. In case of default they can pay them and charge your account. Depending upon how the lender outlines it in the various agreements they could also charge you additional fees and interest. So if you do not have your homeowners' insurance and annual taxes being paid through an escrow account, make sure that you pay them as agreed. Delinquent taxes can become a problem; in fact someone can purchase your past-due taxes from the county and under certain conditions (usually three years worth) they can submit for a deed and take over ownership of your home. So pay your taxes or make sure the escrow company does. The penalties the county charges for late payment of the real estate taxes are usually expensive, something to try to avoid.

Single-Family Homes and Multi-Unit Homes

If you have pledged your residence for security you will typically have a loan agreement, a security agreement, and a mortgage or trust agreement. Many of the same items will be outlined in the truth in lending disclosure as well, which we will discuss further in the regulations section. There will probably be many other documents, which we will outline later. The loan agreement, security agreement, and mortgage inter mix provisions and clauses that describe some of the rights you have and some that the lender has. Not all lenders have the same documents; there are some conforming documents that lenders use, and in fact there are companies that provide those documents to the lender updated periodically according to any new regulations that may have gone into effect. In any event we will try to outline the typical contents. They will discuss the lenders' rights to charge possible fees such as late charges, collection fees, nonsufficient funds fee, annual fees, over the limit fees (which only apply to revolving loans), prepayment penalties, and escrow fees. There are others, but those are the typical fees outlined. They may also outline a default acceleration, which just means they can require you to pay in full once you are in default (or so many months behind). This clause is something that a consumer would probably not be able to abide by or make right by bringing the account current, since they are in default; but they have the clause there for legal purposes. There will also be a section that describes how they intend to credit your account with the payments you make. For example, you have a first mortgage that is a schedule-to-schedule loan, it might describe that they will post any interest earned first, then any late charges due, then insurance (credit insurance), and then to your principal balance. This is important when you are delinquent, as you could lose your insurance coverage and risk not decreasing your principal balance based on these criteria. There may also be a clause that would indicate partial payments are or are not acceptable. There might also be a section that requires you to notify them of any additional lien(s) you might incur in addition to this first lien. When you have rental property pledged, even if it is your home and you rent out other units attached, they might have a clause in the agreement that states they can take over those funds. In case of default they could notify your renter(s) that they must pay their rent directly to them as a mortgage holder. In today's society there isn't much need for the assumptions, which is when someone takes over the loan when you sell the home to them instead of them acquiring a new loan; however, the buyer would still need to pay the seller the difference, so in many cases it is just easier to get the one loan. But there may be a clause that indicates that possibility.

The security agreement and note are in many cases a combined document, and generally the two agreements have the same verbiage and provisions. The mortgage agreement could also have those same policies incorporated, and it would also describe the property with the legal description and how the owner holds title. A husband and wife might hold the property in joint tenancy, which means they have equal rights to the property. They might also hold the property in joint tenancy with rights to survivorship, which means if someone passes away then the other one would own the home solely. There are many different ways to hold title; further research might be needed later. The mortgage should be notarized in order to be recorded. Technically the loan closer should receive identification from you at the time that you signing this document, and they should be a notary; having witnessed you sign, then they sign and stamp the document assuring that it was in fact you that signed the document. The identification you provide should be official, like a driver's license or ID card. Most counties will not record the document, which is the only way for the lender to perfect their lien against your property, if the document is not notarized. The rest of the mortgage's many pages are general in nature, giving the lender rights to the property.

Another term to know is a wrap or blanket mortgage. If you are using more than one property for one loan then it is considered a blanket mortgage. The basic terms remain the same as previously described; however, if you default on "one" you are defaulting on the other one if you have used them both on the same loan. There is no way to separate that obligation without refinancing.

Second Mortgages

Second mortgages are very similar to first mortgages. The only real difference is that they do not have the first position or the same right to reclaim the property. The second is typically not involved in the escrow process, but they do have the same rights to make sure that you pay your homeowners' insurance and force-place insurance. They also hold the same rights to ensure that you pay your annual real estate taxes, and your second mortgage lender can pay them and charge you the same as your first mortgage lender can.

Auto Loans

The security agreement typically outlines that the borrower must maintain auto insurance, and again the agreement will give the lender the right to force-place insurance. Many of these agreements also outline the repossession rights and fees that could apply to that transaction. Once again the agreement will also outline the allowable contract fees such as late charges, nonsufficient funds, and other allowable fees.

Purchase Money for Goods

When you purchase furniture, windows, appliances, and such and then borrow the funds from a lender and sign a contract that outlines that you are using these funds to purchase a product, then you are giving the lender a purchase money agreement. Purchase money agreements are typically one thing that borrowers will have to reaffirm during bankruptcy in order to keep the merchandise. Since these agreements specifically outline the use of the loan funds to purchase exact merchandise, which is itemized in the agreement, you are not allowed this merchandise as an exemption during bankruptcy. In addition they may also outline in this contract their rights to repossess the item(s). These agreements may also allow for fees and default provisions.

Rescission Notices and Mortgage Agreements

We briefly discussed mortgage agreements earlier; the mortgage agreement and the rescission notice generally are the documents that give the lender their rights to the property. The mortgage gives the lender the right, while the rescission notice explains your right to review the terms and documents for at least three business days, and there are states that require longer rescission periods. Rescissions only apply to refinance loans, not purchases of homes. This review period is so that you understand the loan and are certain that you want to pledge your home for this loan. The lender should not contact you during this period to discuss terms unless you asked them to call you about something. The rescission notice is an important document, because if it is not executed properly, you can "rescind" the transaction later. Let's say, for example, that the lender does not give all vested owners (general owners of the property) the proper number of copies of a rescission notice or they forget to have a vested owner sign the document, thus not giving the proper cooling-off period; then the loan become rescindable. Rescindable just means that they do not have a proper lien on the property; the rest of the effects of this would need to be solved through attorneys and the court system. Vested owners are just people who generally own the property; they don't always have to sign the loan or repayment agreement, but all must sign the rescission notice and the mortgage or trust agreement, allowing the lender to have this security interest in the property. If one of the vested owners will not sign the agreement then you probably will not get the loan, as it wouldn't be properly secured. There are other documents that they may need to sign, such as a Section 32 agreement, which generally notifies the borrower(s) of the APR, monthly payment, and in some cases the amount you will be borrowing. This is a federally required document; if your APR is above a predetermined threshold as published by the government monthly then they must disclose this to you. It can also be required if you are paying a certain amount of prepaid finance charges, also referred to as points or loan origination fees. This agreement will also allow for you to consider the loan before you can actually enter into the agreement, again usually three days.

Settlement Agreement or known as HUD 1/HUD 1A

This is a federally required form that typically reiterates some of the same items disclosed in other agreements. Generally this document is at least a disclosure of all fees and disbursements that the loan will transact. If you get on the Internet you can view a blank form on the government site. If you are closing on a purchase property where there is a seller, there will be a section that describes what fees you pay, what fees they pay, and disbursements to the realtor and any other disbursements such as mortgages being paid off, taxes being paid, and broker fees. We will discuss many of these fees in the fee section. This document was designed to ensure that all of the fees and disbursements were disclosed to the consumer in an understanding way.

Arbitration Riders and Wage Agreements

Arbitration riders and wage agreements are not typical for all loans, but many have them. They are normally not a negotiable agreement, meaning that you can elect to sign or not. If the lender has these documents in the document package, they expect you to sign them as part of the loan being granted. The arbitration rider normally outlines how the lender and borrower will settle disagreements. This is generally just designed to cut down on legal costs for the lender, but it also saves the borrower in the same respect. However, in turn it also limits the borrower's right to go directly to court; instead they must go through arbitration and may have to accept the decision(s) made at the arbitration by the arbitrator. Wage assignments are strictly for the lenders. The wage assignment is designed to give the lender the right to collect funds from the borrowers' wages directly. If you sign this agreement and become delinquent, the lender can enact the agreement through your employer. This agreement can be disputed and in many cases not enforced; read the agreement carefully for provisions on how to cease further activities under this agreement.

Closings

With the new wave of technology there are many ways to close loans. You can apply online, receive your papers in the mail, sign them, and they are executed. You can sign at the store-using a credit card, also known as e-sign. You can close loans at a title company or attorney's office, and of course you can still close them at the lending location. Depending upon the closing location, there may be an additional fee for the use of the title company or attorney's office. If they use a courier to deliver the documents you may have a fee for that as well. If you feel uncomfortable with closings, you should have someone there to represent you. The lender, attorney, or closing agent is not there to represent you; they do have legal obligations to disclose the terms of the loans to you, but the agreement generally says by signing it that you understand the contents of it. You don't have to hire an attorney; if you know someone that has financial knowledge, you could ask them to accompany you to the closing. Keep in mind that whoever you invite will know your personal business as the loan closer will not know what not to tell this person. If you are closing on a real estate loan, there are some documents that you could review with someone else prior to the closing. In most states the law requires the lender to allow the consumer to review the HUD settlement at least one day prior to closing. You also receive many disclosure documents in the mail during the application and approval process; make sure you read them all and understand them. If you receive a document that you do not understand make sure you ask your loan representative about the contents of the document(s) that you don't understand.

There are disclosures documents that you will receive throughout the application process on into the approval process that you may need to sign at the closing. We will discuss those disclosures in the regulations section.

Section 4
Chapter 2

Fees

General Fees

No matter what type of loan you have there is typically some sort of fees involved. As you take out the larger loans and move into the mortgage lending the types and amounts of fees increase. All fees that are charged are regulated at a federal level or with even more strict rules by the states. How the financial institution is licensed will determine what laws and rules they must comply with. You can get online with your state regulatory site and review the possible fees, but it is complicated to read through the regulations and try to determine which fees are allowed. One thing to keep in mind is that if you take out a loan with a reputable lender, they watch out to ensure they comply so that they don't have to refund and be charged fines for charging improperly. That doesn't mean that you should not ask or try to ensure the fees you are being charged seem reasonable. Lenders make mistakes too, and while they probably would not overcharge you on purpose it could happen. In some cases and with some lenders the fees can be negotiated and some removed or reduced.

Application Fees

Many lenders charge you for the actual application process and call it an application fee. The general purpose of this fee is to ensure that their loan representatives are not processing paperwork for people not interested in getting a loan, which wastes the lender's time and costs them money. More and more lenders are waiving that fee just to make sure they get far enough into the process to see what they can accomplish for you. With the competitive market it is very likely you could find many lenders that would not charge this fee. Some lenders describe that you will have an application fee, but that they apply those funds to the appraisal or title fees. All that means is that they also want to be sure if they are processing your application and order services such as an appraisal or title work through a third party that they will not be wasting money. Let's say, for example, that you call a lender, they order the appraisal, they come out and appraise your home, and then you decide against the loan. If they charged you for that service they would not lose money, but if they didn't they could lose. Many states will not allow the lenders to collect this fee if the consumer does not take out the loan unless the consumer agreed to pay it if they are approved and then change their mind. So in the application process watch what you sign, as you could be agreeing to pay for costs that you may not want to pay if they do not offer a the loan solution you want. Brokers typically have this type of verbiage in the agreement they have you sign at the onset of the application process. If you are applying for a loan and the representative asks you to sign something so that they can verify your employment or mortgage information, it is OK to sign it once you have read it and completely understand the details within that agreement. It may just be an agreement to release employment and mortgage information, or it may be a combination agreement to release that information and give them the right to charge you for services rendered. Another thing to watch out for is a broker fee. Some brokers have the agreement you sign state that if they get you approved you owe them for the service of them finding you a loan. This is another thing to consider, a broker fee; these fees are for the service of finding you a lender for your specific purpose and amount, plus they assist with the lending process. You need to determine if you can locate a loan on your own or if you need assistance.

As always make sure you know what you are signing and what the documents tell you.

Appraisal Fees and Title Work Fees

These fees are different based on the type of loan you are acquiring and the type of home you own. For appraisal fees they may charge more if you own a multi-unit building; in other words more than one living area and the building has a rental portion of the house or there are more than two separate units. The reason for this is because the lender does typically need more information for that type of lending. They need to know the market better, they need comparisons for other rental properties and the income they bring in, and although most appraisals have maintenance "cost to cure," they for sure need it since "others" live in the property. A cost to cure is the amount that the appraiser estimates it will take to bring the house back to a marketable home. Let's say, for example, that you have a leak in your roof; the appraiser will have to estimate how much it would take to fix that. The reason for this is simple: If the lender has to retake your property later, they want to be able to resell the house. When you are trying to sell a home, it is easier to sell if there aren't a lot of repairs needed. The lender also doesn't want to lend at a higher loan to value if you have extensive cost to cure items. Loan to value just means that if your home is worth $100,000 and you want a loan for $100,000 the loan to value would be 100 percent, which they would not want to do if the cost to cure exceeded, say, $5,000. It is a risk factor that lenders must review the appraisal for and consider how much risk they are willing to enter into. They also review the appraisal to determine how long it will take to resell your property. In many areas the homes sell very fast, while in others it may take six months to sell for the right price. Lenders do not want to loan at 100 percent loan to value in an area where the market takes six months or longer to sell, again a risk factor for them. In today's environment we also find areas that have depreciating values. This means there are many homes that are not worth as much as they used to be worth, for some factor. Most appraisers are reputable, but some are not, so lenders review the comparable property section to ensure that the value the appraiser has set is reasonable and the correct comparables were used and are actually similar to the subject. Most appraisals have a section where they have looked up recent sales for other homes in your area that are similar to your home. In most cases they can find homes that are similar and they adjust for small difference in the homes. However, lenders do not want appraisers to take a three-story home and compare it with a ranch (single-story) home. When people shop for homes, the size and number of rooms are what they shop for, which would certainly be a factor in determining the value of your home. In that same section they will illustrate how many rooms, the square footage of your home, and optional things such as fireplaces, pools, basements, fences, and such. In some markets it is not good to have a pool, because then the amount of people "looking for" a pool would not be 100 percent; but in a warmer climate state it would be more valuable, as more people would be looking to acquire a home with a pool. One final point about appraisals is that there are many types. They could do just a market analysis, which means they would not come inside your home and only go off the general listing information for the homes in your area. They could do a drive by, which would give them a better idea of your home but still not a complete picture. Or they could do a complete appraisal. The more complete the appraisal the more it will cost. One thing to consider about the type of appraisal you elect is that you want to make sure you don't end up with an estimated value that is well above what you believe the actual value to be. The reason for this is you do not want to owe more than your home is worth. You have the right to a copy of any type of appraisal that the lender completes and you pay for. We will not get into appraisals further. If you need more information you may be able to find an article online about appraisals or a book at the library.

Let's discuss title work that would be required. If you are purchasing or refinancing a home there will usually be title work performed. In the lender's policy, which covers the lender in case the title search company did not discover a lien and later that person tries to claim against the property, the title company must provide whatever means is necessary to bring the lender to the rightful position. It could be that the title company would pay off the lien and then they would have the right to go after whoever really owed that money and try to collect. Lenders require this type of title work (search) be done at the time of granting the loan because it is necessary in determining the loan to value and qualifications the consumer has for the loan. If, for example, you represent that you only have a first mortgage and they discover you have a second mortgage also, they would then require you to pay off the first and second mortgage if you are trying to refinance your first mortgage. It could also be that you paid off that second mortgage loan already and somehow the lien did not get released. In this case you will need to contact that lender and ask for a release to be prepared. Sometimes when we pay off liens the company will send you the release that must be recorded at the county court house and the consumer is not aware of this process. When you pay off a mortgage loan, you should look for mail coming from them indicating you paid it off; in some cases they will place the release in that paper work. Many people don't understand about this paperwork and how to handle it. It is important that you file these documents; it is harder to track down the lenders later as they may have even changed their names or been merged with other companies or even closed. There is another type of title policy that you would pay for and acquire when you are purchasing a home. It is called an owner's policy. Basically what an owner's policy does is guarantee the buyer the same rights that the lender has in ensuring you that you hold the property without prior liens that the sellers may have owed. When you are purchasing a property there might have been a lender's lien when the current owner financed the loan, or many other liens. The owner's policy ensures that the title company requires that all prior loans and or liens be paid prior to this purchase transaction completion. Let's say that the builder didn't pay the person who did the landscaping and that person put a lien on the home. If prior liens weren't paid it should not be the new owner's responsibility, so you have this owner's coverage to ensure that you acquire the property free of prior liens. On the settlement statement you will probably see the title work separated; it is all basically the same thing, but there could be more than one entry, one for the search itself and one for the insurance portion. Review them to ensure they do not seem out of line. There may also be a documentation preparation fee in that same section, if you were not previously told about this fee you should ask if you need to pay it, as really it might just additional income lender's charge. Of course it does actually cost them money to prepare the documents, but many lenders will waive that fee to get your business. A notary fee is similar; they typically don't pay extra for a notary, as it is usually inclusive with the closing fee the person closing the loan charges the lender. This is another fee you might have to pay for, the closer; it could be a regular closer or it could be an attorney. Many states actually require closers to be attorneys, and that type of closing is fairly expensive; normally you can't get around that fee, since after all the attorney is required by law.

If you live in a flood zone or not the appraiser will note this on the appraisal, and then the title company, or other source, must also complete a flood certification report for the lender. Of course you will pay for that fee. The appraiser will look up your property at the county, where they keep records on which houses are zoned in a flood zone, and then the appraiser will indicate what type of flood zone you live in. If you live in a flood zone the lender will require you to have flood insurance, which is fairly expensive. If you think there is a possibility that your area has been upgraded to a non-flood zone, you would have to take that up with the zoning committee or the office of records. Sometimes the zoning commission updates their records and reclassifies certain properties in and out of flood zones, but the office of records may not have updated their records yet. For more information on this you could research this further.

Recording, Releases, Stamps, Taxation Fees

When you enter into a real estate transaction there will always be some sort of these recording, releases, stamps, or taxation fees. If it is a purchase transaction the buyers and sellers each pay some of them. If the transaction is a refinance of a prior real estate transaction then you will pay all fees involved. Typically you will have at least one release and one recording fee to pay, since your prior mortgage will need to be released and your new mortgage recorded. These fees are based on the amount the county recorder's office charges to record documents, usually with a base charge and an additional page charge. If you are paying off more than one mortgage, then you will probably have to pay more than one release charge. There are too many variations to describe how all these are charged, but it is enough to know that they are not extensive. Then depending upon what county or state that you live in there may be additional stamp fees. The stamp fees are normally charged based on the amount of the real estate transaction. For example, if your loan will be for $50,000 and the county charges $1.50 per $1,000, then you would pay $.50 x $1.50 = $75.00 for that transaction. The same procedure would apply to any applicable federal stamp fees. There are some cities that charge similar fees, and they normally apply the same way.

When you are entering into a purchase money transaction there is usually what is called a "green sheet" that needs to be completed; this form will outline the amount that you purchased the property for, and taxes will be collect based on that amount and sent to state and federal agencies. All of these fees should be outlined in the settlement statement you receive at closing; you should also receive an estimate in the form of a pre-closing disclosure called the good faith estate.

Inspection Fee and Survey Fees

These are normally fees that are charged for services rendered during the application-approval process. These are not always required, normally just for purchase money transactions. A survey is done to provide a survey to the buyer that describes where the lot being purchased ends and begins. The inspection fee could be several different types; there could be a fee for a pest inspection or for a structural review. These services are normally dictated by the lender as required. You should receive a copy of these reports and retain them for future needs.

Private Mortgage Insurance (PMI)

During the application process this should be discussed if it applies. We briefly mentioned it in a prior section. Private mortgage insurance is just that—insurance, for the lender, that covers the lender in case you default on your loan. This coverage typically only applies to the amount that you finance over the 80 percent. So if you take out a loan for more than 80 percent, many lenders will require you to acquire and pay for this private mortgage insurance. The problem with this type of program is that you often have to prove you have paid the balance down or have in some way increased the value of your home in order to make this insurance not necessary. Normally the only type of evidence you could provide would be an updated appraisal, which costs money, and then you would have to provide that to the correct department and wait for them to review and ensure that they agree that the insurance is not needed. There are some lenders that remove the PMI after a certain time, so review your disclosure to understand what is expected and consider how much to finance based on this additional requirement; Or if there are other options such as a first mortgage at 80% without PMI and a second mortgage for the remainder of your needs. Most second mortgages do not require PMI.

Closing Fees

When you close the loan outside of the lending location, at a place such as the title company or an attorney's office, there will be a closing fee for that service that you would need to pay. There might also be a document preparation fee. These fees may differ by state, due to regulations about whether a company can charge or not. In some states they elect not to charge these fees as the state requires the lender to disclose this fee as a finance charge and the lender would prefer not to.

Annual Fees, Initial Fees, and Advance Charges

These fees normally only apply to revolving loans, mainly credit cards. They require and assess these initially and/or annually. These fees depend upon state allowable fees as well. They charge them to cover the cost of the checks they provide for you to be able to charge again on the account.

Prepayment Penalties and Payoff Request Fees

If you are refinancing one loan into another, they will normally charge payoff request fees, a fax request fee, or even prepayment penalty fees. These fees will be outlined in the payoff request letter that your lender will request in order to pay off that loan. There are often times you can get these fees waived or removed, the effort to do so is worth a try.

Loan Origination, Points, Discount Fees

These are all fees that the lender may charge based upon the type of loan you acquire. These fees are called different things, but they are all the same thing. The financial companies charge these fees to offset the costs of doing business. In some cases, though, they offer the consumer the option of reducing the interest rate they intend to charge by paying a discount fee or points. Let's say, for example, that they will offer you a 7 percent interest rate with no additional discount fees or points, and they will charge you 6.50 percent if you pay a 1 percent discount fee or point. On a $100,000 loan, this would amount to $1,000. If you calculated the loan for a 30-year term at 7 percent, the total repayable would be approximately $239,500, and for a $100,000 loan for 30 years at 6.50 percent the total repayable would be approximately $227,541. So as you can see the $1,000 up front would actually save you monthly payments as well as total finance charges. If you decided to take that same loan for a 15-year term at 7 percent, the total repayable would be approximately

$161,787, and at 6.5 percent total repayable would be approximately $156,798, so once again $1,000 would save you money in the long run. You should always consider your options and if you have the available funds to acquire those options, but don't just pay points and fees without cause.

Paid Outside of Closing Fees

Many lenders allow you to pay fees prior to the closing so that you don't have to come up with the fees at closing. They will normally document this on the settlement statement as POCL or POC. POCL is paid outside of closing by lender and POC is paid outside of closing by consumer.

Escrow Fee

During the application-approval stage you may be asked or required to participate in an escrow account. An escrow account is simply an account that lenders and consumers use to accumulate funds to pay for the annual taxes and insurance for real estate loans. They may offer other items to be escrowed as well. When you set up this type of account the lender will calculate an estimated amount that you will need to pay into this account monthly in order to have the correct amount when the taxes and insurance come due. If your taxes and insurance increase during the year, your lender will normally just pay them and create a negative escrow balance and then re-estimate your monthly payment (raise your monthly payment) to make up for the prior year and attempt to create enough for the next payment(s). Escrowing your taxes and insurance is a good idea unless you often have the ability to come up with a large amount of cash to pay these fees during the year, or you are disciplined enough to save the money yourself.

Odd Days' Interest (Additional Days)

Many lenders charge the consumer when they close the loan for the "odd days' interest." Odd days' interest is just the extra days between your closing date and the first of the month, if that is the date your monthly payment will be due. Most lenders want all their due dates to be the first so they charge the consumer for the extra days to bring the payment to the first. So if you close your loan on the twenty-ninth there are 30 days in that month they will need to charge you for one or two days depending on how many days are in the next month as well. It is a small charge and typically disclosed on the settlement statement. However it is important to understand that closing towards the end of the month will often allow you to have less closing costs.

There are many types of fees as you can see from this section. You need to review all the fees they intend to charge you and all the fees they disclose that they are charging you.

Section 5
Chapter 1

Regulation Z Truth in Lending (TIL)

The Truth in Lending Act was originally enacted in 1968. Its purpose was to protect the customer and allow them to compare one lender to another. This act has had many additions to it since its inception. This regulation relates to the protection of the customer in various forms or disclosure requirements for the lender(s) as well as giving the customer the right to cancel certain transactions under certain conditions. Also described in this act is the need for lenders to disclose terms that are understandable to the public; they should also disclose what they normally charge. For example, if they normally charge $400 for a settlement fee and they disclose to you that it will be $200 that is not a fair estimation. As we have discussed, the lender must disclose the finance charges that you will occur for the transaction (loan) that you are signing for. The way the government defines finance charges is to consider a cash transaction versus a loan. The charges that you would normally pay for under a cash transaction are not finance charges, such as sales tax, licensing-title (such as with an auto purchase).

We have discussed the many fees associated with a loan; the majority of those are finance charges, and as stated previously some states (government of) consider different items finance charges that other states may not. One of those would be an attorney fee for closings; many states consider this just a fee and not a finance charge fee as it is best for the consumer and maybe even required; however some states do define this fee in the overall finance charge fees. Another one might be appraisal fee; this is required in order to get a real estate loan, and the lender does not generally profit from this fee so it usually is not included in the finance charge definition.

Items to Disclose

The truth in lending disclosure should have the consumer's identity (usually their name and address), the lender's identity, loan type, the amount financed, itemization of the amount financed, finance charges, annual percentage rate, payment schedule, including number of years and the payment for the amount financed disclosed, and total number of payments. Then lenders need to disclose other items such as variable rate features, demand feature(s), prepayment penalty, late charges, security interests and fees associated with recording that interest, insurance availability, and if elected, assumption policy, required deposit, and reference to contract. When the lender discloses the APR and you have a closed-end fixed-rate loan, this is simple: Your loan should react as the disclosure indicates. However, if you have a revolving or adjustable-rate loan, then it is only a picture in time as the terms of those loans generally change over time. For variable-rate loans you would need to disclose minimums and maximums (ceilings and floors). The APR is basically the cost calculated over one year's time, the annual percentage rate. So if your loan has a 10 percent fixed interest rate for a $100,000 loan set for 30 years with $250 in fees and you are paying 1.5 percent ($750) prepaid finance charges, loan origination fees, or discount fees/points— whichever term they are using; it is all basically "figured" or "added" into the rate to arrive at a APR—then your APR would not be 10 percent; it would be 10.24 percent approximately. What this means is that you are paying the 1.5 percent ($750), plus the $250 in fees over 30 years. So I calculated the fees and prepaid finance charges into the $100,000 loan spread out over 30 years. Another way to look at it is the $1,000 worth of fees and charges amount to .24 percent of the 10.24 percent APR. What does that mean? If you calculate a loan with a 10 percent interest rate versus a 10.24 percent interest rate, you would find that higher APR will cost more. The APR in this case is more about costs that you paid at the closing; the APR does not mean that the loan will cost you 10.24 through the life of the loan if you actually pay the fees at closing, but if you finance them then you are paying for them for the life of the loan. That is what this regulation has generally required lenders to disclose.

Many lenders choose to use only one form to disclose all of this information, and some use several to separate out certain aspects of the loan, such as insurance. The lender should always disclose all fees prior to the loan close, not just at the closing, so that the consumer has time to review and decide. There are other regulations that indicate lenders can use the GFE (good faith estimate) at application time and then supply the TIL at the closing if the real estate transaction is a refinance or other than a purchase. For the purchase of a home transaction, the regulation requires the TIL disclosure at least three days prior to consummation, since the GFE does disclose most of the items that the original regulation intended for the consumer to use as a comparison between lenders so they may use just one form that is for the purpose of disclosing the TIL and GFE items. Since a GFE is not generally required for revolving lines of credit, they require certain terms of how the loan will work at application time, which could be a TIL or HELOC (home equity line of credit) disclosure, such things as we have previously discussed like minimum and maximum interest rates, adjustment periods, minimum advance amounts, termination of the credit limit, and over the limit charges. There are stipulations that say the writing must be so big and that they must box certain things in a specific order so that the consumers can easily read and understand the terms.

Credit Card Rules

As described earlier there are other sections of this regulation, either added or within the original set of rules. One of those is a provision for credit card practices—to include the handling of billing and billing error resolution procedures, issuance of a credit card must be authorized—advertising disclosure requirements, credit limit termination provisions, and the consumer liability for unauthorized uses limitations.

Credit card companies have many practices outlined in this regulation section to follow. There must be certain items disclosed at application or solicitation time, such as APR, grace period for purchases, membership fees or annual fees, and all other fees related to a specific transaction. Some of the other fees might be a cash advance fee, late payment charge, over the limit fee, and balance transfer fee. There must also be an explanation of how finance charges will be calculated. Consumers generally understand that they will receive a billing statement monthly, but that is also a requirement of this regulation, and many of those same items that are disclosed at inception must be disclosed on the statement as they apply. There is an actual billing rights disclosure that the creditor usually puts on the back of every billing statement. The credit card company must also disclose if any terms of the agreement will change, such as an insurance provider, the minimum payment, or a billing cycle. The creditor must remind the consumer once annually that they will have an annual fee, usually one month before they actually charge it.

Billing Issues

If the consumer believes that there is a billing error, they must notify the creditor within 60 days, and then the creditor has 30 days to acknowledge receipt of the dispute and must resolve the dispute within two additional statements, not to exceed 90 days. A billing dispute may arise for the following reasons: unauthorized debt, insufficient identification or wrong information of charges, improper crediting of payment, computational errors, wrong transaction dates, mistake in dollar amount of an item, and statement mailed to the wrong address. There are certain circumstances where the consumer can withhold payment of the disputed items, but I would not advise it, as it could hurt your credit. If it turns out to be the company's fault you can always get a refund.

Electronic Communication

In this regulation there are also provisions for electronic communications. Basically it states that the creditor must have permission in order to deliver disclosures via the Internet.

High-Cost Loan Disclosure

This disclosure provision applies to loans that are typically of a higher interest rate. This is an early disclosure, or at least designed to be a disclosure that you receive at least three business days prior to the actual signing of the loan. This is a rescission period of sorts, where you have the option to review these specific loan terms and decide if this is the right loan for you. This applies to a consumer's residence in the first lien position where the following applies: the APR is greater than 8 percentage points over the treasury securities yield as published on the fifteenth of the month prior to the application, or the total points and fees payable for the transaction exceed 8 percent of the total loan amount or an amount specified in this regulation (Z). As of 2003 it was $499.00, subject to change annually. For loans that are subordinate liens or second or third mortgages, the yield cannot exceed 10 percent over the treasury securities yield. So if the loan you are about to obtain does go over these provisions then the lender is required to give you a disclosure that states the APR, total amount borrowed, and regular payments; the consumer then has the right to review that document for three business days prior to the actual signing of the loan.

There are other provisions within this portion of the regulation as well. If they are providing you with this high-cost loan, your debt to income ratio must not exceed 50 percent, and they cannot consider future income raises, interest calculations cannot be based on the rules of 78, no negative amortization, no balloon payment if the term is less than five years, and there cannot be a refinance of another high-cost loan within one year of the original financing of the prior high-cost loan. This regulation also notes that lenders cannot provide a revolving loan (open-end) loan to the consumer to avoid this provision. There are a few other nuances, but those are the basics.

Right of Rescission

The last portion of this regulation we will review is the right to rescind, or cancel. If an account is secured by your principal residence the lender must give you the right to cancel the transaction within three business days of the closing. You will be provided this disclosure at the closing. This does not apply to home purchases. This rescission period is designed for you to be able to review the terms of the agreement and decide if the loan is truly what you want. Under the regulation the creditor must supply two copies of this notice to each person who has the right to rescind this transaction; typically this is anyone who has a right to the property by way of ownership. No disbursements of the loan should occur until this three-day time period is completed. The days are normally calculated using Saturday as a business day, but not Sunday, and do not include federally recognized holidays. If you decide not to go through with the loan you need to execute the rescission notice; note that the notice can be given in writing via the fax, in person, or in the mail. If you mail the rescission notice to rescind you run the risk of being outside of your rescission period. It is better to send it overnight with some sort of confirmation that you have sent it to the business. The notice itself usually describes how to cancel as well.

I have described the basics of this regulation; there are many other provisions and rules that lenders must follow. As always you are welcome to do further research. As stated earlier many of the regulations overlap and can create a situation where you seem to have several disclosures that say the same thing. Be careful to read them all anyway, as there may be a slight difference. The disclosures are all designed to inform the consumer, not to overload the consumer with paperwork; however, many times it ends up being an overload of paper. This leads to one final note: Generally lenders are required to keep all documents and disclosures in connection with the application(s) or transaction(s).

Although I don't want to get too deep into this subject, please remember that someone who tries to sell you something, like a vacuum cleaner, in your home must also give you a rescission notice and a time frame for you to be able to cancel that transaction. Due to the nature of sale, the fact that there could be pressure to purchase an item in order to get an individual to leave your home.

Section 5
Chapter 2
Regulation B & ECOA

Equal Credit Opportunity Act

This act, of equal opportunity for all to obtain credit, originally only prohibited discrimination based on sex and marital status. It was later revised to also cover race, color, religion, national origin, age, or whether one's income is in part or all made up of public assistance program(s). In essence the lender must consider all items equally without regard to the above discrimination classes. The act also calls for the lender to describe and explain the reasons for denial in writing within 30 days of the application. The consumer is entitled to a free copy of their credit bureau report if in any way the credit report was a determining factor for the denial. The lender cannot discourage any applicant from applying for credit in a way that could imply that the creditor is discriminating.

Fair Housing Act

The Fair Housing Act basically mirrors the equal credit opportunity act prohibited basis except with additional guidance for lenders to ensure equal opportunity in regards to real estate lending. This act does not limit the amount of damages that the government can award under this act if not complied with.

Regulation B General

There are several ways the government reviews for this type of discrimination. The regulation in conjunction with the lender defines at what point the loan inquiry becomes an application; this may not be important to you as a consumer. They review the lender's credit scoring to ensure that it does not discriminate against the prohibitive basis in itself. This regulation was amended in 2003 to allow for institutions to self-test themselves to ensure compliance with this regulation. They can review their own applications to evaluate if there are any discriminating factors. If you feel that you have not been given an equal opportunity to credit you can seek assistance from the ECOA or FHA.

The regulation calls for how companies evaluate their application based on income. The lender must review all income equally, such as a married person trying to apply for a loan without their spouse: The actual income for that one person must be considered the same as if it were the combination of incomes from two parties applying.

Section 5
Chapter 3
UDAP & HMDA

Unfair and Deceptive Acts or Practices (UDAP)

http://www.federalreserve.gov/BoardDocs/Press/
bcreg/2004/20040311/attachment.pdf

http://www.consumerlaw.org/publications/manuals/content/samples/
M5udap_814-817.pdf

This regulation applies to unfair acts, such as charging excessive fees or actions that generally treat the consumer in an unfair manner. So if you charge $5,000 in fees, did the consumer receive at least that much in some other form of benefit? Most lenders have some sort of analysis to determine what is called "Net tangible benefit." Some of those tests include but are not limited to monthly savings, cash out to the consumer for more than the fees being paid, pay-off debts, or home improvements.

This regulation was enacted to protect the consumer against deceptive practices. For our purposes this law applies generally to lenders but could also be used against a product producer. If a lending institution says "No closing cost" and then there is a charge, that type of behavior is said to be misleading and therefore deceptive and against the law. The law is open for government interpretation, but generally the government responds to consumers who feel they were promised one thing and then ended up with another, also known as the bait and switch. This act was not put in place so that the consumer is not responsible for their actions, but more so that they are not misled, that it is reasonable for one to expect what they are told they are getting.

The above is the general basis of the regulation; please see the web sites for further information. For the consumer to issue a compliant you would need to determine which agency regulates the company in question.

For lenders it is generally the FDIC, FTC, OCC, or DFI. Your states attorney general's office can assist you in determining who to contact.

Home Mortgage Disclosure Act (HMDA) Regulation C

http://www.ffiec.gov/hmda/history2.htm

HMDA was created to ensure that lenders were servicing their community and not discriminating on any basis. In simplistic terms each lending institution must report certain information about the loans that are applied for to the government for analysis, and the government will review and determine issues through their audit processes. Have you ever been asked your ethnicity? It could be so that the loan officer could document for HMDA.

Many regulations cross over others: HMDA and ECOA have similar implications.

Section 5
Chapter 4
FCRA & RESPA & SSCRA &FDCPA

Fair Credit Reporting Act (FCRA)

http://www.ftc.gov/bcp/conline/pubs/credit/fcrasummary.pdf

http://www.ftc.gov/bcp/menus/consumer/credit/rights.shtm

Over the past couple of years there has been much activity with this regulation as fraud and identity theft increase. A consumer has more rights to receive one annual copy of their credit and more rights to dispute what is reported within the credit report. The reporting agency should make sure what they are reporting is accurate and or corrected upon evidence of errors. As we have discussed in other sections, a consumer's credit score can make a difference in what loan and interest rate one qualifies for. Therefore, it is important for this information to be supplied and monitored by the consumer; thus the reason for this enactment.

For more information see the web sites provided.

Real Estate Settlement Procedures Act (RESPA)

http://www.hud.gov/offices/hsg/sfh/res/resindus.cfm

http://www.hud.gov/offices/hsg/sfh/res/respa_hm.cfm

The purpose behind this regulation is so that the consumer is well informed about their transaction as it relates to fees and relationships as they apply to the transaction. Not all real estate loans require the same disclosures, but almost all of them require some sort of consumer awareness.

There are generally three disclosures that apply for **RESPA** requirements: HUD Special Booklet (mostly for first mortgage purchase transactions), GFE (good faith estimate), and mortgage servicing disclosure. Of course there are other requirements—see the official web site for details—but generally these three are the main consideration of the regulation.

The booklet mainly deals with purchase transactions and tries to inform the consumer about what to expect within the transaction. One should receive this at the time of application or mailed within three business days.

The good faith estimate is just that, an estimate of what the costs will be generally with the type of loan being applied for, and it must be received at time of application or sent within three business days after a full application is received. This document is critical and should really be reviewed carefully by the consumer. If you do not understand a fee or item on the disclosure you should ask your lender and maybe even seek additional qualified advice. If you see fees arranged in the form of a range like $1,000–2,000 you should certainly question your lender as to what the actual fees will be. The general idea is for the lender to disclose what they normally charge so to have such a large range may not be acceptable under the terms of this regulation.

The mortgage service disclosure is generally to let the consumer know about the lender's practices, such as how often they sell their loans to other investors or if they transfer servicing. One should receive this at the time of application or mailed within three business days.

A whole book could be written on the basis of RESPA, but above is the basics. See the government web site or legal counsel for further information.

Soldiers & Sailors Civil Relief Act (SSCRA)

http://www.access.gpo.gov/uscode/title50a/50a_10_1_1_.html

Just to give a brief high-level overview, this act was created so that military persons called to duty wouldn't have to worry about their bills while defending the nation. There are provisions that allow a POA (power of attorney) to be used for items that need to be handled financially while they are in active service. There are provisions for lenders to accommodate lower interest rates and/or deferment of payment during these times as well, based on the qualifications of the regulation. Please see the government web site for further information regarding the details.

Fair Debt Collection Practices Act (FDCPA)

http://www.ftc.gov/bcp/conline/pubs/credit/fdc.shtm

Much like any regulation, an entire book can be written about it; however, we will just give you the general basics. The government says that there are certain fair collection practices and some inappropriate ones. For example, a collection agency is restricted further than the actual lender as they are acting in someone else's behalf. Another example is that there are certain hours that are acceptable to call. For example, calling at midnight might only be OK for someone who does not work the day shift. Even though the regulation was intended for collection agencies, most lending institutions have adopted the policies and follow them fairly closely. As is common in the regulations, a debt collector cannot represent something that is not true. An example might be if a debt collector knows that the amount owed is too small to file a lawsuit, yet they say they will; this is not allowed. They also can't call your brother and ask for your phone number representing that you won the lottery and that they are a representative of the lottery.

Another thing to remember is you cannot be harassed for monies owed. You can ask for them not to call you at work, you can even ask them not to call you at home, but if you don't accept calls you might force them to seek out other remedies allowed by law to collect, such as court.

If you want more information see the government web site.

Glossary-Definition Sources:

http://biz.yahoo.com/f/g/

http://www.investopedia.com/

http://www.fraudaid.com/Dictionary-of-Financial-Scam-Terms/

http://www.ny.frb.org/education/define.html